Lost and Found in *Translation*

Research on Korea

Edited by Marion Eggert, Eun-Jeung Lee and Jörg Plassen

Volume 2

Zur Qualitätssicherung und Peer Review der vorliegenden Publikation

Die Qualität der in dieser Reihe erscheinenden Arbeiten wird vor der Publikation durch einen Herausgeber der Reihe oder durch einen externen Gutachter geprüft.

Notes on the quality assurance and peer review of this publication

Prior to publication, the quality of the work published in this series is reviewed by one of the editors or by an external reviewer of this series.

Eun-Jeung Lee / Hannes B. Mosler (eds.)

Lost and Found in *Translation*

Circulating Ideas of Policy and Legal Decision Processes in Korea and Germany

PL ACADEMIC RESEARCH

Bibliographic Information published by the Deutsche Nationalbibliothek
The Deutsche Nationalbibliothek lists this publication in the Deutsche Nationalbibliografie; detailed bibliographic data is available in the internet at http://dnb.d-nb.de.

Library of Congress Cataloging-in-Publication Data
Lost and found in translation : circulating ideas of policy and legal decision processes in Korea and Germany / Eun-Jeung Lee, Hannes B. Mosler (eds.).
pages cm. — (Research on Korea, ISSN 2196-0895 ; volume 2)
ISBN 978-3-631-64908-4 — ISBN 978-3-653-03961-0 (E-Book) 1. Political planning—Korea (South) 2. Political planning—Germany. 3. Policy sciences—Korea (South) 4. Policy sciences—Germany. 5. Translating and interpreting—Political aspects—Korea (South) 6. Translating and interpreting—Political aspects—Germany. 7. Law—Korea (South)—Language. 8. Law—Germany—Language. I. Lee, Eun-Jeung, editor of compilation. II. Mosler, Hannes B., 1976-
JQ1725.A55P64458 2015
320.60943—dc23
2014046782

This work was supported by the Academy of Korean Studies of the Republic of Korea (AKS-2009-MA-1001).

한국학중앙연구원
THE ACADEMY OF KOREAN STUDIES

ISSN 2196-0895
ISBN 978-3-631-64908-4 (Print)
E-ISBN 978-3-653-03961-0 (E-Book)
DOI 10.3726/978-3-653-03961-0

PL Academic Research is an Imprint of Peter Lang GmbH.

Peter Lang – Frankfurt am Main · Bern · Bruxelles · New York · Oxford · Warszawa · Wien

This publication has been peer reviewed.

www.peterlang.com

Contents

Eun-Jeung Lee and Hannes B. Mosler
Introduction 7

CHAPTER 1 - TRANSLATION AS AN ANALYTICAL CONCEPT 15

Eun-Jeung Lee
(1) Transfer of Knowledge as a Matter of Translation 17

Paul Stubbs
(2) Translating Welfare Assemblages in the "New" Eastern
Europe: Re-domaining the Social? 31

CHAPTER 2 - TRANSLATIONS IN SOCIAL POLICY MAKING 55

Yun-Tae Kim
(3) The Making of the Welfare State in Korea: Policy
Discourses and Strategies 57

Myung Joon Park
(4) Micro-Policy Translation and Policy Entrepreneurship
in the Transformation of Korean Welfare Capitalism 73

CHAPTER 3 - THE TRANSLATION OF LEGAL
NORMS AND IDEAS...89

Seog-Yun Song
(5) The Transplantation of the German Constitutional Provision
on Political Parties in South Korea 91

Hannes B. Mosler
(6) Legal Translations "Made In Korea" 115

Appendix 161

Eun-Jeung Lee / Hannes B. Mosler

Introduction

"Policy moves, across time and space and in a number of other ways, too. It is made in words, and words which move are translations."
(Freeman)

It has by now become almost commonplace in academic literature to note that processes of circulating knowledge, or *epistemai*, as well as dynamic transformations of institutions occur all over the world, and that they are more and more interactively connected to one another. There is a burgeoning research literature on internationalizing, globalizing, and supernationalizing ideas, knowledge, policies, and institutions. The field of operational research, in particular, has recently seen some very fruitful endeavors dealing with the question of how to describe, analyze, and explain the worldwide diffusion of ideas and knowledge on policy issues.

As is well known, previous academic literature attempted to approach these phenomena by understanding them as processes of "copying," "transferring," "teaching," "learning," "transmitting," or "transplanting." Recently, such approaches to analyzing the dissemination of policy ideas and policy decisions – in the form of policy transfer, policy learning, legal transplantation, and knowledge diffusion – have been challenged by the analytical concept of policy *translation*. The rationale behind this post-positivistic, conceptualized perspective is to improve on existing approaches by widening the scope of analysis to include dynamics and mechanisms that have not, so far, been properly addressed in spite of forming part of the dissemination process. Most of the still scarce literature on the translation concept bases its argumentation on a constructivist understanding that emphasizes aspects such as interactivity, intersubjectivity, and contingency. In so doing, this literature tries to go beyond understanding the complex process of dissemination merely as a phenomenon of "donating," "receiving," or "arbitrarily utilizing" policy ideas, norms, and laws. It speaks of the importance of *context* in trying to understand the manner in which ideas travel and in which they become modified, particularly when it comes to the manner in which their journey is connected to, and shaped by, wider political struggles.

What is *policy translation*, and what is it good for? What contribution can the concept of "translation" make to explaining the emergence of policy ideas and their travel across borders? Most importantly, how effective can it be in analyzing actual cases of policy dissemination? The chapters of this book will deal with these questions both on a general, theoretical level and within the context of policies and laws that have traveled in actual fact, namely between South Korea and Germany. South Korea is widely considered a typical example of a reforming country "receiving" policies and ideas from "more advanced" countries. It thus promises to be an especially interesting case for testing the applicability of the translation approach.

This book is based on contributions to a conference titled *Lost or Found in Policy Translation?*, which was held in Berlin from March 29 to 31, 2012 under the auspices of the Institute of Korean Studies at Freie Universität Berlin. The conference formed part of a research project called "Circulation of Knowledge and the Dynamics of Transformation: Korea and Beyond," a project jointly conducted by the Institute of Korean Studies at Freie Universität Berlin and the Institute of Korean Studies at Ruhr-University Bochum, with funding provided by the Academy of Korean Studies (AKS)[1]. The project is led by professors Dr. Eun-Jeung Lee (Berlin), Dr. Marion Eggert, and Dr. Jörg Plassen (both Bochum).

The conference aimed to analyze the phenomenon of various actors in various contexts and settings adopting different interpretations of one and the same idea, with a particular focus on examining the degree to which the concept of "translation" could prove useful to such analysis. The first chapter of this publication sheds light on existing conceptions of policy translation, on their implications, potentials, and limits, while the second chapter examines the dynamics of the Korean social welfare system through the analytical lens of "translation." The third and final chapter of this book focuses on the dissemination and implementation of legal ideas, policies, and norms as a form of "translation."

I

Eun-Jeung Lee's contribution opens the book's discussion by dealing with the introductory, yet fundamental, topic of "Transfer of Knowledge as a Matter of Translation" in the context of unification policies in Germany and Korea. Discussing the exchange of knowledge and ideas on German unification between Korean and German politicians, scientists, and (other) policy actors, Lee challenges the notion that the difference in the situations of the two countries stands in the way of mutual cross-fertilization between Korea and Germany. More specifically, she sets out to examine whether it is "really true that there is no such

1 AKS Overseas Leading University Program for Korean Studies, AKS-2009-MA-1001.

thing as a successful transfer of policy between two countries with different traditions, institutions, and cultures."

Having introduced some historic cases of successful intercultural transfer of knowledge and policies, Lee discusses the existing academic discourses on policy transfer. She then looks into the concept of "policy translation," characterizing the act of translating a policy as a process consisting of four steps: problematization, selection, reduction, and mobilization. In her conclusion, Lee states that once policy transfer is interpreted not as a simple act of transfer, but rather is seen from the point of view of cultural translation, intercultural policy transfer becomes a real possibility, which, in the case of Korea, opens up the prospect of drawing on the German experience of unification in a meaningful manner.

II

Paul Stubbs' contribution "Translating Welfare Assemblages in the 'New' Eastern Europe: Re-domaining the Social?" adapts the notion of "assemblage" so as to enrich the concept of translation in the literature on policy decision making. Referring to authors of various strands, Stubbs submits that the concept of "assemblage" is homologous to that of "translation," thereby deepening the notion to include meanings such as "complex becoming and multiple determinations […] sensitive to time and temporality in the emergence and mutation of phenomena that should never be reified as final or stable states." He attempts to develop a vocabulary, epistemology, and methodology that emphasizes "the interactions, the complexity, and the liminality of encounters between actors, sites, scales and contexts." According to him, the concepts of "policy translation" and "assemblages" capture well the ways in which policy meanings are being constantly transformed, translated, distorted, and modified.

Stubbs proceeds in three steps: first, he builds on Kingfisher's ideas, whilst questioning whether the ideas of "horizontal" and "vertical" movements can be rescued from their underlying objectivist ontology, and discusses in broad terms the usage of this framework in social policy and social welfare; second, he discusses aspects of the social dimension of the "great transformation" in Central, Eastern, and Southeastern Europe, revisiting some of his own, and others', contributions; and lastly, he makes some general remarks regarding future research agendas and enters into a tentative discussion on how to build "an ethics of translation" into social and development policy interventions.

In his contribution "The Making of the Welfare State in Korea: Policy Discourses and Strategies," *Yun Tae Kim* deals with the competing discourses and strategies that have influenced the development of welfare systems and the expansion of welfare expenditure in South Korea. He argues that social policy in Korea has developed the unique characteristics of the welfare state, and that it has been transformed into a more comprehensive welfare state since the late 1990s. Kim then goes on to evaluate the institutional consequences of welfare reform in Korea and analyzes the underlying nature of welfare state transformation in relation to Western experiences. Finally, he considers Korea's future prospects of sustaining its developmental social policy goals and of providing all its citizens with social security.

Kim's overall assessment of the situation in South Korea is that, while European countries have moved closer to the East Asian productivist tradition of social spending, there is, in fact, pressure in East Asia to expand social spending in a manner reminiscent of directions previously taken in Europe. According to him, recent developments in South Korean welfare institutions have raised issues with a view to equality and social justice. A considerable proportion of the workforce presently find themselves in unstable, non-standard employment, and a high proportion of unemployed people and pensioners remain uncovered by national pension systems. It should be noted that social spending is relatively low and directed in ways that have little impact on poverty among older people or people of working age. The problems involved in addressing inequality suggest that social investment strategies need to be set in a context where there are benefits to support the poor of working age, the elderly, and disabled people.

In a contribution titled "Micro-Policy Translation and Policy Entrepreneurship in the Transformation of Korean Welfare Capitalism," *Myung Joon Park* attempts to apply the analytical concept of "translation" to decision-making processes in South Korean welfare policy. To this end, he has carried out an empirical analysis of the emergence of the Employment Insurance System (EIS), a social insurance program established in the wake of democratization designed to guarantee the livelihoods of workers in times of unemployment. As the first comprehensive mechanism to protect workers against unemployment, its establishment had epoch-making implications for the institutions of Korean welfare capitalism. Park analyzes the discursive contests over the creation of the EIS in what can be understood as an act of macro-policy interpretation. Analyzing the process of emergence of the EIS from the perspective of policy translation, his study focuses on the role of policy experts, i.e., those who were exposed to the experiences of other advanced countries and who accordingly developed an alternative concept for reform. According to Park, the activities of these policy experts can be understood as a form of policy entrepreneurship. In other words, the experts' role as policy translators in establishing the EIS contained elements of the kind of role typically played by policy entrepreneurs.

For his study, Park conducted intensive interviews with three experts in the field of labor markets, including a policy entrepreneur who had played a critical role in creating the EIS. In so doing, Park intended to demonstrate not only that the entrepreneurship of policy experts was crucial in creating the EIS, but also that it formed part of a more comprehensive act of policy translation. In addition, Park explores the utility of the translation approach for analyzing Korean welfare capitalism as part of a new democracy in East Asia. He concludes by finding that the EIS could not have been established without the special efforts and acts of policy translation undertaken by a number of policy entrepreneurs. Among other things, these entrepreneurs creatively changed the name of the program, set up a unit for research and discussion, persuaded opponents to join the program by utilizing their networks, and drew up their concept for reform only after having gathered and analyzed an exhaustive amount of information on the systems of other advanced countries.

III

In "The Transplantation of the German Constitutional Provision on Political Parties in South Korea," *Seog-Yun Song* analyzes the adoption of the Korean constitutional provision on political parties in the year 1962 as a way of exemplifying the kind of role that the transplantation of Western constitutional provisions played in the modernization of developing countries. In doing so, Song does not content himself with merely comparing and contrasting the respective provisions in the Korean and German constitutions, but takes a closer look at the methods of comparative legal research, in particular at the notion of "legal transplantation." His approach therefore reflects the necessity to recognize the fact that law is not independent from social development, and that, accordingly, "law in action" should not be overlooked when scrutinizing the phenomenon that is the dissemination of legal ideas and norms.

In analyzing the differences between the German and Korean laws on political parties, Song points to the rather striking differences in the historical circumstances prevailing at the time of their respective creation, namely at the end of the 1940s in the case of Germany, and at the beginning of the 1960s in the case of Korea. While Germany had lost a war and subsequently put behind it years of cruel dictatorship, Korea had experienced liberation from Japanese colonial rule, followed by the Korean War, and had then turned towards dictatorship. To Song, the basic tenet of German post-war democracy was that democracy could never be value-neutral since the parties of both the extreme left and the extreme right had to be kept under equal control. His analysis of the relevant debates in the German parliament reveals that this rationale served to balance the constitutionally guaranteed freedom of political parties with their constitutional responsibilities. In Korea, on the other hand, the constitution of 1962 proclaimed party monopoly in parliamentary and presidential elections, and the Political Parties Act of the same year laid down very rigid requirements for the registration of political parties as a way of "modernizing" politics. In other words, the political realities and needs of Germany at the end of the 1940s were rather different from those prevailing in Korea at the beginning of the 1960s. Even so, Korean legislators made explicit reference to German law in their drafting of the Korean provisions on political parties.

Based on his analysis, Song concludes that, on the whole, the transplantation of the German constitutional provision on political parties into the Korean context in the name of "political modernization" did not help to build a democratic party system. In fact, he submits, one can hardly deny that individual elements of the imported provisions and theories were overemphasized in a manner apt to legitimize the authoritarian party system. Against this background, Song argues that the danger of such rather crude transplantation could be reduced through a constitutional design in line with socio-legal constitutional thought.

Concluding this book, *Hannes B. Mosler's* contribution "Legal Translations 'Made In Korea'" applies the analytical concept of "translation" to the generation and alteration of legal ideas and norms in Korea. Mosler takes the Korean constitution and its provision on political parties, together with other Korean laws related to political parties, to be the most prominent examples in this respect. Having discussed, both in theoretical and empirical terms, the metaphor of the "transplantation of laws" as widely used in legal scholarship, he goes on to contrast "transplantation" with "translation" as a heuristic device for explaining the circulation of legal ideas and norms. More specifically, Mosler reduces the metaphorical concept of "translation" to an operational method for empirical analysis, demonstrating the advantages of the "translation" metaphor and the method derived from it by applying the latter to a number of representative cases.

Mosler maintains that a conceptual shift from the notion of transplantation to that of translation has the potential to further invigorate the already growing literature on policy translation. While he also argues for the usefulness of metaphors such as "legal transplant," "legal irritant," or "legal transformation," he claims that the translation metaphor is conducive to an epistemologically informed appraisal of the phenomena associated with the circulation of legal ideas that offers greater reach and depth than the more established metaphors. Mosler concludes by submitting that Korean policy and law have, translated or not, always been "Made in Korea," and that the translation metaphor as an analytical tool is capable of providing valuable clues to identifying, and ultimately meeting, the challenges ahead in making policy and laws in Korea.

Acknowledgements

This book could not have been written without the help and support of many individuals and institutions. We extend our gratitude to them all. In particular, we are grateful to the Academy of Korean Studies (AKS), for without its support, neither the conference nor the publication of this book would have been possible. In addition to the contributors to this volume, we would also like to thank the following individuals for serving as chairs and discussants and providing helpful comments at the conference: Jang-Hee Yoo (Seoul), Wolfgang Heinz (Berlin), Farhad Muktharov (Baku), and Gebhard M. Rehm (Munich). Last but not least, we want to express our gratitude to Irene Maier for undertaking the formidable task of copy-editing the final version of this book.

Chapter 1
Translation as an analytical concept

Eun-Jeung Lee

(1) Transfer of Knowledge as a Matter of Translation

Abstract This chapter deals with the introductory, yet fundamental, topic of transfer of knowledge as a matter of *translation* in the context of unification policies in Germany and Korea by discussing the exchange of knowledge and ideas on German unification between Korean and German politicians, scientists, and (other) policy actors.

1. Introduction

Whenever "unification" is discussed in Korea, German unification and its potential lessons for Korea are bound to be mentioned. Almost equally inevitably, however, it will be argued that the situations of both countries are too different for the German experience to be able to provide Korea with any guidance. All research on German unification eventually runs into this wall. But is it really true that there is no such thing as a successful transfer of policy between two countries with different traditions, institutions, and cultures?

In reality, intercultural policy transfers have occurred quite often in human history. Furthermore, in some cases at least, they have been rather successful. Confucius taught that one can learn even from a stone from another mountain, which means not only that one can learn from others, but also that one should actively strive to do so. It is possible to learn from experiences of all sorts, failures included. If this is true, then what are the necessary conditions for intercultural policy transfer to be successful? Is there a "golden rule" for policy transfer?

For my part, I will attempt to explain intercultural policy transfer as a matter of "translation."

In the first part of what follows, I will mention some historic cases of successful intercultural transfer of knowledge and policies. Then, in the second, I will go on to make some remarks about the existing academic discourses on policy transfers. Based on the concept of "translation," I will proceed to look into the meaning of "policy translation." Finally, in part four, I will make some observations about the characteristic properties of policy translation.

This paper is only a first step on the way to a long-term research project. Any criticisms or suggestions will be gratefully received.

2. The "transfer" of knowledge and policies as a historical phenomenon

The transfer of knowledge and policies has a long history in East Asia, going back to a time long before the first contacts with the Western world. In the cases of Korea and Japan in particular, there was a great deal of cultural and policy transfer from China.

As they built their own state systems between the 4th and 7th centuries – in the case of Korea, during the period of the Three Kingdoms (Koguryo, Shilla, Paekchae), in the case of Japan, under the rule of Shotoku Taishi – both Korea and Japan adopted and implemented the Chinese political and legal system. It was through this process that the East Asian Chinese character culture was formed.[1] The Chinese system of government became a model for the newly empowered rulers of Japan and Korea. But the Chinese model was not simply adopted as it stood. The resultant political systems of Japan and Korea were similar to, yet at the same time quite different from, the Chinese system of government.

These cases from ancient history are examples of successful policy "transfers." They are not limited to the transfer of the Chinese system of government, but also include the import of Confucianism and Buddhism. The social, political, and economic conditions of the receiving countries had a determining influence on the process of adopting and implementing Chinese culture and institutions. Korean and Japanese societies and polities were radically transformed and started developing in new ways, while the umbilical cord to China remained uncut. In Korea, the downfall of the Koryo Dynasty was closely related to the import of neo-Confucianism from China, which had given rise to a new literati group, the so-called *sadaebu*, and had helped propel the founding of the Choson Dynasty.

In East Asia, transfers of policy and knowledge mostly took the form of implementations of the more advanced Chinese systems. Prior to the arrival of Western missionaries and merchants in China toward the end of the 16th century, East Asia developed within its own cultural sphere, devoid of any significant contact with the West or other civilizations. Once contact with the West was established, East Asia proved intellectually open to Western influences, particularly to the influence of Jesuit missionaries, who were readily accepted on the strength of their knowledge of science and technology. Some of them even rose to high positions in the Chinese government.

Similarly, Japan also actively adopted new, Western forms of knowledge, including them under what it called *rangaku* (Dutch studies) (Horiuchi 2003). In

1 See Nishijima Sadao's concept of an East Asian "kanji cultural sphere": (Sadao 1983).

17th century Korea, intellectual and political conflicts emerged around the merits of Western knowledge. Under the influence of Chinese books on Christian thought, Catholic groups were formed, even though Western missionaries were yet to set foot in Korea.

At that time, Europe was also intellectually quite open to new ideas. Philosophers such as Leibniz and Christian Wolff took an active interest in the political system of China and integrated Confucian thought into their own philosophies. They maintained that the Chinese political system, in particular the system of state examinations for civil servants, ought to be implemented in Europe (Lee 2003).

As this example shows, contacts between East Asia and Europe were not based solely on the transfer of scientific knowledge and systems from Europe to East Asia, but rather took the form of a mutual exchange. This, of course, was rarely recognized, mostly because the intellectual mood prevailing in late-Enlightenment Europe was decidedly Euro-centric. Particularly after James Cook discovered the Australian continent in the late 18th century, Europeans felt assured that no civilization was superior to their own (Rüdiger 2012: 140).

Thereafter, Euro-centrism was firmly established. After the Opium Wars, European superiority could no longer be doubted, and East Asia fell under the yoke of European oppression and exploitation. In the course of the 19th century, the superiority of European civilization even became a self-evident truth in the eyes of most East Asian peoples, in particular their elites. From then on, in the West and in the East alike, the transfer of knowledge was seen as a one-way transfer from West to East. And indeed, from the middle of the 19th century onwards, transfers of Western institutions and knowledge to East Asia reached considerable volume.

Wherever they could, the European imperial powers imposed their rules on the established systems. In East Asia, fierce debates arose about how to respond to European imperialism. Three distinct approaches emerged: 1) advocating modernization along the lines of the Western model; 2) demanding renewed commitment to, and a revitalization of, one's own traditions; and, finally, 3) advocating a two-pronged strategy that called for the "preservation of indigenous values while at the same time adopting know-how and technical knowledge" from the West.[2] In the second half of the 19th century, this latter strategy gave rise to the notion,

2 Comparable reactions could be observed in other cultures confronted with European expansionism, as Dieter Senghaas describes in his book *Zivilisierung wider Willen*: (Senghaas 1998: 14).

still influential in present-day East Asia, that what matters is combining "Eastern thought and morality and Western technology and instruments."[3]

Hostilities between proponents of the differing approaches were associated with sometimes bloody political struggles.[4] Yet by the end of the Second World War, most countries had come to accept Western political systems, including communism. Furthermore, non-Western societies undertook great efforts to learn from Western experience in the domains of economic policy, law, welfare policy, and the like.

In present-day Korea, debate about knowledge transfer tends to focus on lessons to be learned from recent processes of transformation in Germany and Eastern Europe. There is, however, another strand of that debate which highlights the issue of the transfer of the Korean "model" of economic development to other countries such as Vietnam.

3. Academic debates on "transfer" and translation

As seen in the previous section, there are various historical cases of knowledge and policy transfer between different cultures. And this kind of process is a phenomenon that will continue independently of how academics choose to study it. For a long time, it was predominantly referred to as one of "transfer". In the case of East Asia, it tended to be characterized as a process of "learning" or "implementation", or as a case of deriving a "lesson" (Bennett and Howlett 1992; McLaughlin 1987). Although "learning" and "implementation" suggest "one-way transfers", nobody has taken issue with this terminology, and it has therefore remained generally unchanged from the 19th century until the present. Korean efforts to investigate the unification of Germany and the transformation of Eastern Europe are no exception in that they have also tended to employ a terminology of "lessons" and "learning." However, it is also commonly argued that since Germany and Korea have different cultures, Korea cannot simply adopt German unification policies (Han 2012).

This skepticism has much to do with terms such as "transfer," "lesson," and "implementation." Etymologically, the word transfer (Latin *transfero*) means "to

3 The concept is known by different names in China, Japan, and Korea respectively - as *zhongtixiyong*, *wakonyôsai*, and *dongdoseogi*. Prior to 1868, the Japanese spoke of *tôyô dôtoku seiyô geijutu*.

4 In Japan, the faction that favored reforms and Western-style modernization prevailed in 1868. Reformers in Korea and China, by contrast, faced much greater difficulties. Reform efforts in 1884, 1894–1896, and 1898 all met with failure. The protagonists of these reform movements fled to Japan or the U.S., or were executed.

move or pass from one place, person or thing to another," or "to convey the impression of (something) from one surface to another."[5] In this sense, "transfer" does not refer to a reciprocal activity. Indeed, the expression smacks of mechanical monocausality, of a process that does not allow for any adaptations to accommodate specific situations or circumstances.

This concept of "transfer," then, does not allow for any reciprocity, nor for a modification of particular roles or characteristics. As a result, whenever one speaks of intercultural policy "transfer," there will be someone pointing out the impossibility of a direct, one-to-one transfer. This goes to explain why there are, in fact, many who oppose attempts to apply the results of research on German unification to Korea almost by instinct.

In any culture, at any period of time, attempting to adapt policies or knowledge is a task far too complex and interactive in nature to constitute an act of simple "transfer." The process of state-building in Korea and Japan during ancient times, as well as the implementation of Western systems during the Meiji period in Japan, cannot be explained solely through the concept of transfer in that they were *creative* processes.

Whether new forms of knowledge and types of institutions gain authority and acceptance will not depend on any intrinsic authority, but on whether they are successfully implemented in their respective new environments. One example of a successfully implemented policy is that of introducing Western-style short hair for men through a number of "Short Hair Edicts" passed in East Asia in the late 19th century.[6] The fact that short hair came to prevail as the dominant hairstyle

5 Webster's Dictionary.

6 The three East Asian countries took different routes to introducing short hair for men as a political act. The Japanese elite of the Meiji period was first to believe that in order to attain the Western civilization's level of advancement, one ought to copy the West in matters of appearance, too. Japanese soldiers and policemen therefore began to dress in Western-style uniforms and wear their hair short. The emperor and high-ranking politicians equally lead by example, with low-level officials and the common people following suit. While there was no outright coercion, the traditional hairstyle came to be considered as "barbaric," and those insisting on wearing their hair the traditional way were soon derided as "barbarians." Unlike Japanese men, Korean men were formally ordered to cut off their traditionally long hair and in spite of their fierce protest found themselves forced to do so. Opposition to the 1895 Short Hair Edict was partly due to the fact that it had been issued and enforced under pressure from Japan, which by that time made no efforts to conceal its imperialist ambitions. Yet despite initial strong resistance, short hair gradually took a hold in Korea and ultimately became a hallmark of the "modern boy." For Chinese men, the obligation to wear their

for men cannot be put down to any particular strength of short hair in and of itself, but instead to the fact that the elites of Japan, and of East Asia as a whole, came to consider wearing one's hair short as a sign of Western modernization.

A similar case took place in Europe in the early 19th century, when students clamoring for reforms at Hambach Castle ceremonially cut off their "Zöpfe" in a sign of protest. While there is no direct link between these two events, both signified a move towards modernization. As the social and political contexts of Japan, Korea, and China were different, the short hair policy was implemented differently in each country.

Indeed, a proper understanding of *context* is crucial to successfully transferring a policy between two different contexts or frames. Failure to grasp differences in context is likely to complicate, or altogether stifle, efforts to transfer policy, as demonstrated by recent Korean debates about potential lessons to be learned from German unification. When Germany was unified in 1990, hopes for a reunification of Korea initially grew. But soon afterwards, public opinion in Korea rapidly turned around, mainly on account of estimates of the expected cost of unification. As the media began to report details of the costs incurred in the process of German unification, the issue of costs became a topic of paramount importance in Korean public discourse. Would a financially weaker Korea be able to bear such a huge burden?

However, if the specific conditions prevailing in Korea had been properly taken into account, the question of the costs of unification would have lost much of its alleged importance and would certainly not have justified a radical turn in public opinion. To begin with, more than half of the costs of German unification were related to social expenditure. As the social welfare systems are much less developed in Korea, costs related to social expenditure would never reach German dimensions. Moreover, the burden of the costs of Korean unification, however heavy it might turn out to be, would surely be mitigated by the fact that unification would finally put an end to the tremendous burden the current division of the peninsula represents to each of the countries, as well as to their respective allies.

This simple example shows that it is necessary to carefully investigate, and spell out in detail, the specific social, economic, political, and other conditions capable of affecting a potential transfer. Intercultural policy transfer is not a matter

hair short came with an order in the wake of the Revolution of 1911. These differences in the way short hair for men was imposed in China, Japan, and Korea are very telling of the complexity of East Asian "modernity."

of a one-to-one transfer of "pure" policy, but a creative act that requires an understanding of what measures are appropriate to the specific context of implementation. In this sense, transferring a policy requires an act of *translating* from the specific setting of one culture or country to that of another (Freeman 2009; Buck and Shahrim 2005; Greenhalgh and Wieringa 2011; Hagström and Johnson 2005; Lütz 2007).

4. The meaning of "translation"

The term "translation" has traditionally been used in literary and cultural studies, but not often in social science, and especially not in political science. As I am using it here, "translation" does not relate to the translation of words, but instead to "cultural translation" in the Benjaminian sense of the term.

By coining the term "cultural translation," Walter Benjamin went beyond the traditional term "translation," which simply referred to the translation of words. Cultural translation can be defined as an active process of interpreting and transforming other cultures within a specific historical context; it is neither an equivalent exchange of meanings between different cultural texts, nor a mediation of meanings from a transcendental position. Benjamin's theorization of translation is productive in that it frees translation from having to be a parasite on the original, and instead allows it to occupy an autonomous position – after all, what the translator aspires to translate is not the original text but what Benjamin calls "pure language," an unrepresentable "idea" that is "potentiality" inherent in, but not reducible to, the original (Benjamin 1923).

For Benjamin, cultural translation goes beyond a pure translation of the text; the text should instead be translated in the sense of its cultural context. His views were actively adopted in the cultural studies field from the moment cultural translation became a theoretical issue. In the theory of cultural translation, translation is defined as a particular case of intercultural communication with the purpose of overcoming the wall separating different cultures. The starting point for cultural translation theory is the hypothesis that cultural differences, such as differences in traditions, values, and ways of thinking, make intercultural communication impossible (Bassnett and Refevere 1990).

Benjamin's "translator" plays a central role in the process of cultural translation. This is because, as Kim Hyŏn-mi notes: "In cultural translation, the context under which the translation takes place and the translator, depending on who they are, can either bring about an equal relationship between two cultures, or create a hierarchical relationship between them." (Kim 2009: 25; my translation) In a similar vein, Lydia Liu emphasizes that "the crucial thing [...] is not whether translation between cultures is possible (people do it anyway), or whether the 'other' is knowable, or even whether an abstruse 'text' is decipherable, but what practical purpose or needs [...] bring an ethnographer to pursue cultural translation." (Liu 1995: 2)

A transfer of policy, then, should be understood as an act of "cultural translation." Any policy transfer requires the translator to have a specific goal in mind. Any act of "transferring" policy results in a new translation that must be able to stand its ground in whatever happens to be its immediate context – which is why the original policy must be modified in order to adapt it to different political configurations in different general circumstances.

Of course, "translation" is as much a metaphor as "transfer" is, which leads to problems when describing cultural and social practice. Nevertheless, we can agree, as Freeman has stated, that the concept of translation is better suited to explain the act of adopting a particular policy than the rival concept of "transfer" is.

The term "translation" makes the uncertainties that affect any "sign," as an instrument of communication, clearly visible. These uncertainties do not only affect intercultural communication, but also communication *within* a particular society or culture. It is in reference to this that Freeman contends: "We communicate by means of signs (words and pictures, sounds and images), that is, by choosing or making representations of what we mean. But the relationship between the sign and what it signifies is neither determined nor mechanical: what things mean or represent is a matter of convention (a social construct) and it is invariably inexact. Understanding may come to be shared, but it cannot be identical. This fundamental epistemological uncertainty, this requirement that every utterance be accompanied by some hermeneutic move on the part of the reader or listener, is a source of innovation and creativity as well as error and failure. Translation makes this uncertainty explicit." (Freeman 2009: 440)

It is in this sense that structural linguists such as Saussure understand translation to be "a sign which stands for a sign, a representation of a representation or a representation." In actual fact, the concept of translation means not only "the replacing of terms in one language with those in another," but above all "a substitution of one set of relationships or associations with another." (Freeman 2008: 5) Translation is a performative "articulation," and it is in this sense that the concept is used by Stuart Hall and by Ernesto Laclau. It is "the work of bringing two (or more) things into relation with one another. For such relationships are not essential or given: they have to be made and maintained, or 'performed.'" (Law 1999) Such relationships can be agonistic and differential, but also antagonistic. In this sense, the notion of translation is a "dual movement of (re)presentation and (re)association," which "draws attention to the change, adaptation, mutation and transformation which takes place in all instances of communication or transfer." (Freeman 2008: 12)

Freeman explains that by describing the adoption of policies as "translation," the following advantages are gained (Freeman 2008):

- Policies are described as social constructs with a narrative structure rather than as given objects or instrumental practices with fixed meanings;
- Adopting a policy is described as a practice of communication hampered by "border problems" (in the form of breaks, gaps, or abysses in communication);
- Adopting a policy is described as a dynamic process rather than a clear-cut, one-off operation;
- It is also described as a collective process with multiple authors and contexts;
- And, finally, it is described as part of a wider context that reflects the dynamics of political struggles.

5. The characteristics of intercultural policy transfer as an act of cultural translation

As Freeman has indicated, policy is essentially a social construct and the result of a dynamic process brought about through the practice of communication. Processes of intercultural policy transfer, for their part, can be said to consist of three elements: two separate cultural contexts with their respective policy structures, and a person wanting to transfer a particular policy from one context to the other. Applying the theory of cultural translation to this constellation, we can identify the original policy, as created in the relevant source culture, on the one hand, and the policy inspired by this original policy, to be applied in what might be thought of as the "target culture," on the other. Conceiving of policy transfer in this way, the person transferring a policy is essentially a translator, and as such both a reader of the source culture and a writer of the target culture.

Diagram 1

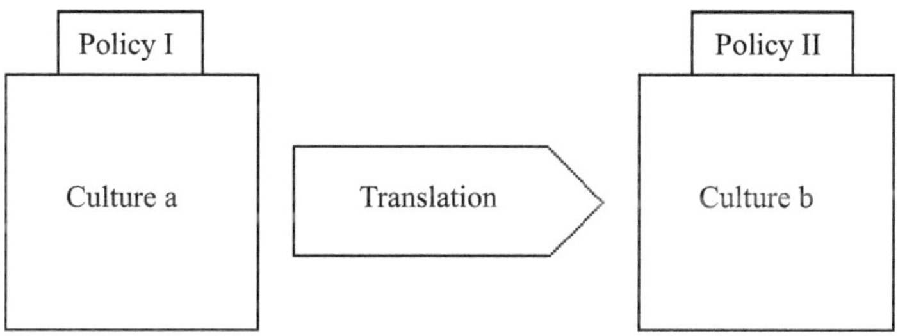

The internal structure of the policy decision process is not dissimilar. Within the policy decision process, one can discern: first, the key actor, who plays an important role; second, the phenomenon that has been identified as the problem needing to be solved; and, last, the competitive relationship between the various discursive coalitions that emerge in the process of finding a solution.

Hannes Mosler has proposed the following diagram to explain this process (Mosler 2011):

Diagram 2

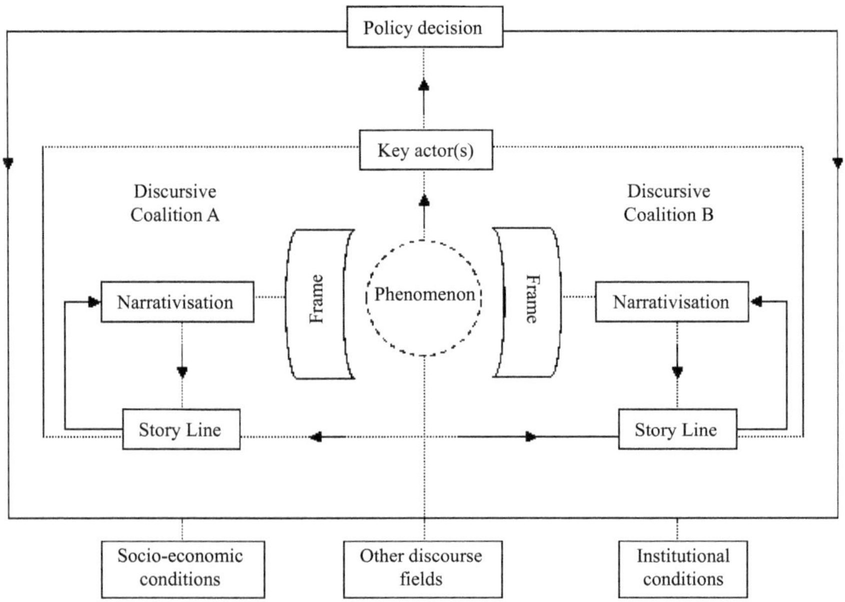

The discursive coalitions each work towards understanding the phenomenon identified as a problem, create their own storyline in the process of trying to find a solution to this problem, and, ultimately, develop what may be called their "discursive frame". We can refer to this framing as a kind of "translation." Next to cases where a policy decision is made and then "handed down" by the key actor, there will also be cases where a policy decision "rises up" from among the competing discourses put forward by the various discursive coalitions. Which discourse is able to take the top spot in the competition will depend on which coalition has come up with the most convincing framing for, or translation of, the phenomenon at hand.

The decisive role in policy transfer as an act of cultural translation falls, of course, to the translator. Historical cases of successful intercultural policy transfer relied on the fact that the translator succeeded in linking together the policy decision processes that shaped the source language text with those that determined the target language text. What is important to note here is that the act of translating in the course of a policy transfer is clearly different from other acts of cultural translation. It may be said to be a process consisting in four steps: problematization, selection, reduction, and mobilization.

Problematization: In the first place, the translator needs to understand the problem in its wider context. In the case of the Korean and Japanese Short Hair Edicts, the starting point, from the point of view of the reformers, was to recognize the underdevelopment of East Asia and the unequal relationship between Europe and East Asia.

Selection: Once the problem has been identified, the search for a solution can begin. This process includes examining the experiences of other countries. At the end of the 19th century, the countries of East Asia believed that in order to overcome the West, it was necessary to create a policy geared towards building *a rich land and a strong army*. For that purpose, they sent delegations to Europe and America, the Iwakura delegation of Japan being most famous among these. The members of the latter traveled to America, England, France, and Germany, and let themselves be inspired by what they thought could be successfully applied to the case of Japan.

Reduction: As a result of the translator identifying a solution, a process of reduction begins. This is the point at which is it possible to engage in misinterpretations of the source language text. We can find two prominent examples of reduction from the late 19th century. One concerns the Short Hair Edicts, the other the establishment of Shinto as the state religion in Japan. In the case of the Short Hair Edicts, short hair was equated with Western modernity. In the case of the transformation of Shinto into a state religion, the Japanese elites looked to Europe, believing that Christian churches, as representative bodies of state religions, had played a major role in European modernization. They accordingly turned Shinto into a state religion and actively destroyed thousands of Buddhist temples and monasteries.

Mobilization: The ideas gleaned from another country's policy experience are then mobilized for the discourse surrounding the policy decision to be made in the target country. At times discursive coalitions engaged in one and the same discourse will attempt to mobilize examples from different policy experiences. One example of this is the current Korean discourse on welfare policy, in which various discursive coalitions instrumentalize the German, British, American, Japanese, and Scandinavian cases respectively to support their positions.

This process can be graphically expressed using the diagram below. In the left part of the diagram, a policy decision is shown to result from the discursive competition in the source country or source context. This policy and its implementation are interpreted by a translator in the light of conditions prevailing in the target country or target context. The translator then introduces this interpretation of the policy into the discourse surrounding the policy decision to be made in the target country or target context. Since conditions prevailing in the target country or target context are bound to be quite different from those prevailing in the source country or source context, such intercultural transfers of policy cannot, by their very nature, constitute one-to-one transfers of policy.

Diagram 3

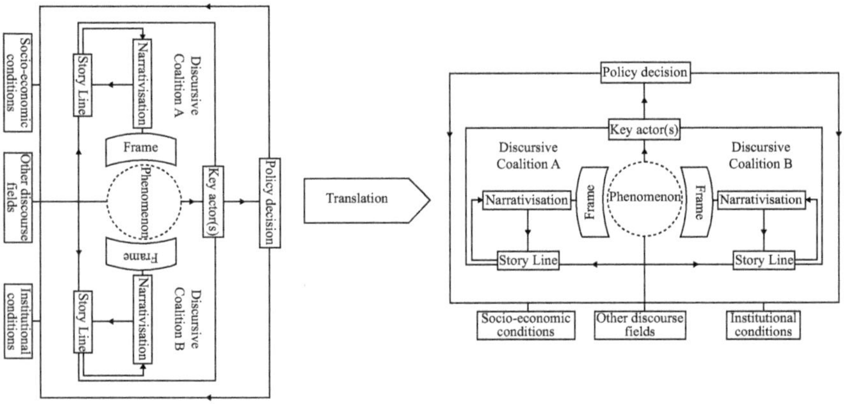

6. In lieu of a conclusion

I am skeptical about skeptics who believe that nothing can be learned from the experience of German unification. This is because, as I hope to have demonstrated, intercultural policy transfer conceived of not as a simple act of transfer, but rather as an act of cultural translation, does have the potential to become viable and meaningful. It would therefore, I submit, be desirable for further research to set out to examine the necessary conditions for successful policy transfer.

References

Bassnett, Susan and Andre Refevere. 1990. *History, translation, and culture.* London: Print Publisher.

Benjamin, Walter. 1923. *Charles Baudelaire, Tableaux Parisiens. Deutsche Übertragung mit einem Vorwort über die Aufgabe des Übersetzers, französisch und deutsch.* Heidelberg: Verlag von Richard Weißbach.

Bennett, Colin J. and Michael Howlett. 1992. "The Lessons of Learning: Reconciling Theories of Policy Learning and Policy Change." *Policy Sciences,* Vol. 25, No. 3. 275–294.

Buck, Trevor and Azura Shahrim. 2005. "The Translation of Corporate Governance Changes across National Cultures: The Case of Germany." *Journal of International Business Studies,* Vol. 36, No. 1. 42–61.

Freeman, Richard. 2009. "What is 'translation'?" *Evidence & Policy,* Vol. 5, No. 4. 429–447.

Freeman, Richard. 2008. "Policy moves: translation, policy and politics." *MS unpublished.* University of Edinburgh.

Greenhalgh, Trisha and Sietse Wieringa. 2011. "Is it time to drop the 'knowledge translation' metaphor? A critical literature review." *Journal of the Royal Society of Medicine,* Vol. 104, No. 12. 501–509.

Hagström, Bo and Björn Johnson. 2005. "The Translation Perspective as an Alternative to the Policy Diffusion Paradigm: The Case of the Swedish Methadone Maintenance Treatment." *Journal of Social Policy,* Vol. 34, No. 3. 365–388.

Han, Un-suk. 2012. "Rezeption der soziokulturellen und wirtschaftlichen Integration nach der deutschen Wiedervereinigung in Süd-Korea." Paper presented at the workshop on "German Unification and Lessons for Korea", Berlin, December 22, 2012.

Horiuchi, Annick. 2003. "When Science Develops outside State Patronage: Dutch Studies in Japan at the Turn of the Nineteenth Century." *Early Science and Medicine,* Vol. 8, No. 2. 148–172.

Kim, Hyŏn-mi. 2009. *Kŭllobŏl sidae-ŭi munhwabŏnyŏk [Cultural Translation in the Age of Globalization].* Seoul: Tto hana-ŭi munhwa.

Law, John. 1999. "After ANT: complexity, naming and topology." In *Actor Network Theory and After,* edited by John Law and John Hassard. Oxford: Blackwell, 1–14.

Lee, Eun-Jeung. 2003. *"Anti-Europa". Die Geschichte der Rezeption des Konfuzianismus und der konfuzianischen Gesellschaft in Europa von der frühen*

Aufklärung bis zur Gegenwart. Eine ideengeschichtliche Untersuchung. Münster: Lit.

Liu, Lydia. 1995. *Translingual Practice: Literature, National Culture, and Translated Modernity*. Stanford: Stanford University Press.

Lütz, Susanne. 2007. "Policy-Transfer and Policy-Diffusion." In *Handbuch Governance*, edited by Arthur Benz, Susanne Lütz, Uwe Schimank and Georg Simonis. Wiesbaden: VS Verlag, 132–143.

McLaughlin, Milbrey Wallin. 1987. "Learning from Experience: Lessons from Policy Implementation." *Educational Evaluation and Policy Analysis,* vol. 9, No. 2. 171–178.

Mosler, Hannes B. 2011. "Tamnonbunsŏkchŏk chŏpkŭn-ŭro koch'arhae pon chedogaehyŏk-ŭi chŏngch'aek kyŏlchŏng gwajŏng-e taehan yŏn'gu. Han'guk chigudang p'yeji sarye-rŭl chungsim-ŭro (Diskursanalytische Studie zu politischen Entscheidungsprozessen institutioneller Reformen in Südkorea mit Fokus auf die Abschaffung der Parteiorganisationen auf Wahlkreisebene)." PhD diss., Seoul National University.

Rüdiger, Axel. 2012. "'Die Revolution ist […] die Revolution' - Georg Forster über Sprache, Politik und Aufklärung." In *Georg-Forster-Studien XVII*, edited by Stefan Greif and Michael Ewert. Kassel: Kassel University Press, 121–171.

Sadao, Nishijima. 1983. *Chugoku Kodai Kokka to Higashi Ajia Sekai (The Ancient State of China and the East Asian World)*. Tokyo: Tokyo daikaku shuppansha.

Senghaas, Dieter. 1998. *Zivilisierung wider Willen (Involuntary Civilization)*. Frankfurt a.M.: Suhrkamp.

Paul Stubbs

(2) Translating Welfare Assemblages in the "New" Eastern Europe: Re-domaining the Social?

Abstract The author of this chapter adapts the notion of "assemblage" so as to enrich the concept of translation in the literature on policy decision making, and argues for developing a vocabulary, epistemology, and methodology that emphasize the interactions, the complexity, and the liminality of encounters between actors, sites, scales and contexts.

1. Introduction: Escaping the orthodoxies of social policy studies

One of the paradoxes of the academic study of social policy, at least in the developed world, has been that, despite the inherent multi-disciplinary nature of its endeavor, it is still rather narrow in focus, limited in scope and range, and simplistically normative in moving from analyzing "what is" to suggesting "what should be." Many of the most important recent "turns" in the social sciences, be they "cultural," "discursive," "interpretative," "spatial," or "post-colonial," have tended to be ignored, dismissed, or misunderstood by the main body of social policy scholarship. Recognition that the subject matter of social policy is no longer solely the nation state, and less still the particular Northern and Western European "welfare state" form that it was assumed, wrongly as it turns out, would likely remain in place forever, has hardly stirred the pot. It has led less to a fundamental rethinking, than it has to a new field of "comparative," "international" or "global" social policy studies that, on the whole, represents little more than a "'scaling up' of the objectivist knowledge of nation states to include supra-national actors" (Lendvai and Stubbs 2009a: 224) framed in terms of a taken-for-granted hierarchy of fixed, static, "levels": local, national, regional, and global. There is no need to dwell on the causes of this, although I share John Clarke's suspicion that it relates to a self-image as both "applied," aspiring more to be "useful" for welfare workers than "academic"; and "junior," in the sense that complex concepts are best left to others and, hence, arrive late, if at all, and invariably in highly simplified form (Clarke 2004: 3).

One vignette from my own journey towards a more critical, post-structuralist[1] approach to social policy stands out, in retrospect, as being of particular significance. As a part-time research fellow on the "Globalism and Social Policy Programme" (GASPP), under the directorship of Bob Deacon, I attended the third GASPP Seminar on "International NGOs, Consulting Companies and Global Social Policy: Subcontracting Governance?" in Helsinki in December 1999.[2] I presented a rather rough and unfinished paper on "Globalization, Humanitarianism, and the Culture of Social Policy." In some ways, it updated the rather orthodox presentation of the Yugoslav and post-Yugoslav story I had written as chapter 5 of "Global Social Policy" (Deacon, Hulse and Stubbs 1997: 153–94). It did so under the strong influence of a "new wave" of Croatian anthropologists working in the Institute of Ethnology and Folklore Research, in Zagreb, where I lived, on issues relating to "War, Exile, and Everyday Life" (*cf.* Jambrešić Kirin and Povrzanović eds. 1996). The paper also borrowed very much from the work of authors such as James Clifford (especially Clifford 1997) and Katherine Verdery (*cf.* Verdery 1996). I had also just read "Welfare and Culture in Europe: towards a new paradigm in social policy" (Chamberlayne *et al.* (eds.) 1999). In their different ways, these connections, and my experience "on the ground" as an activist/practitioner/researcher in the post-Yugoslav space, led me to want to explore further the "cultural" conditions and lived experience of welfare as a set of nested and contested social relations. The attempt was not well received by Deacon ("clever but irrelevant" were his words, as I recall), or by other GASPP researchers and associates, who were troubled by my apparent retreat from the goal of "global social justice." The criticism should not have been unexpected given Deacon's strong views on the problems of both the "cynical gaze of Marxism" and "the paralyzing gaze of postmodernism" (Deacon *et al.* 1997: 7). I received support, both publically and privately, from two other attendees at the event, Janine Wedel and Jeremy Gould, who drew my attention to emerging work on an anthropology of policy (*cf.* Shore and Wright (eds.) 1997) and the possibilities of "studying up" within a kind of multi-level ethnography (*cf.* Gould 2004; Wedel 1999; 2004).

The Helsinki paper was published eventually as "Globalization, memory and welfare regimes in transition: towards an anthropology of transnational policy transfers" (Stubbs 2002). The title itself shows that I was not yet fully capable

1 I have been known to add two other "posts" to situate my work: "post-Marxist" and "post-colonial." I resist, rather strongly, being labelled as "post-modernist" or, simply, "constructivist."

2 http://gaspp.stakes.fi/EN/seminars/gaspp3.htm (accessed 1 March 2012).

of escaping from the conceptual straitjackets of "welfare regimes" and "policy transfer" ideas to a more liberating framework, both intellectually and practically, in terms of ideas of "welfare assemblages" and "policy translation." The statement that the story of global welfare reform is "complex and contradictory," accessible through ethnographic methods underpinned by an "anthropology of policy" (Stubbs 2002: 328), while rather vague, was at least a marker for future work. The encounter with the work of Noémi Lendvai (*cf.* Lendvai 2004) and of John Clarke (Clarke 2004) was crucial in refining these half-formed ideas into a more substantive body of work, leading to ongoing collaborations with both of them (*cf.* Lendvai and Stubbs 2007; 2009a; 2009b; Clarke and Stubbs 2011). In addition, the Interest Group on the Anthropology of Public Policy (IGAPP) of the American Anthropological Association,[3] under Janine Wedel's stewardship, has been more than tolerant of three non-anthropologists, allowing us to explore these issues in two panels "Beyond Policy Transfer: transnational translations and the reconfiguring of technocracy and politics" (in 2009) and "Tracing Policy: translation and assemblage" (in 2011).

In some ways, the latter panel shows how far a framing of (social and/or development) policy in terms of "translation and assemblage" has moved, with the panel organizer, Catherine Kingfisher, succinctly summarizing the debate thus:

> This session brings together two strands of thinking in the anthropology of policy to explore the movement of policy both horizontally, across sites, and vertically, from policy-making centers down to the street level. The first is the framework of policy production and implementation as translation. Most frequently used to highlight the selectivity, agendas, and power plays at work when policies developed in one location are transferred to another, the framework of translation can also provide insights into how policy is taken up and engaged with both by those who apply it and those who are its targets. A second approach is provided by the concept of assemblage, which serves to highlight the situated, cut-and-paste nature of policy, underscoring the piecemeal, experimental, and constantly unfolding nature of both policy production and implementation. As policies are translated and assembled, new formations emerge, in the process erasing or accentuating received perspectives and practices (Kingfisher 2011a).

This paper tries to do three things. Section II builds on Kingfisher's ideas whilst questioning whether the idea of "horizontal" and "vertical" movements can be rescued from their highly objectivist ontology, and discusses in broad terms the usage of this framework in social policy and social welfare. Section III discusses aspects of the social dimension of the "great transformation" in Central, Eastern,

3 http://aaa-igapp.net/ (accessed 1 March 2012).

and South Eastern Europe, revisiting some of my own, and others', contributions. Section IV makes some general remarks regarding future research agendas and enters into a tentative discussion on how to build "an ethics of translation" into social and development policy interventions.

2. Translating welfare assemblages: Reconceptualizing social policy

The concept of "translation" has, itself, travelled far beyond linguistic theory, being adopted and adapted in different ways, within policy studies, cultural studies, anthropology, and post-colonial studies (Lendvai and Bainton 2011). Like the concept of "assemblage," it serves to remind us of the fluid and dynamic nature of the social world, encompassing "displacement," "dislocation," "transformation," and "negotiation" (Callon 1986). Translation is not a process of arbitrary "free association"; rather, it is a deeply politicized process which is concerned with "the building, transforming or disrupting of power relations" (Sakai 2006: 71–2). Insofar as "(p)olicy is made in words, and moves" (Freeman 2009: 431), so that "meaning can be lost in translation, or made by it" (*ibid*: 432), the process through which dominant discourses are reproduced is never automatic but always involves adaptation and change, "reconstituted in another place, in another form, with different implications" (*ibid*: 434).

As suggested elsewhere (Lendvai and Stubbs 2007, 2009b), the idea of "policy as translation" questions, above all, the concept of "policy transfer" as a linear process of policy diffusion or transplantation, challenging assumptions of an objectified or commodified knowledge "extrapolated from its context" (Yanow 2004: 15). Indeed, a sociology of translation provides a way of exploring "the interrelation of discourse and agency" (Newton 1996: 731), since translation requires translators, acting within "actor-networks" of humans and non-humans (actants) (*cf.* Latour 1987). "Translation" is a crucial part of an anthropology of policy which emphasizes the "messiness and complexity of policy processes" (Shore and Wright 2011: 8), as a set of imaginaries or narratives "moving through time and space" non-linearly, with attempts to embed policies as authoritative, normative forms (the idea that "there is no alternative"), opening up new spaces of contestation ("there is a crack in everything, that's how the light gets in"[4]). The attempt to render policies as universal through the "re-transcribing" (Venn 2006: 82) of socio-economic, administrative, bureaucratic, and political practices, usually viewed in

4 Lyrics taken from the Leonard Cohen song "Anthem" from the album "The Future" (1992).

terms of a transnationalizing, even globalizing, "neo-liberal" discourse (*ibid.*), has limits to its logic, tending to produce "hybrids, paradoxes, tensions, and incompatibilities" (Clarke 2004: 94). While policies exist within "domains of meaning" (Shore and Wright 2011: 1), the study of the creation of "new alignments" or "new social and semantic terrains" (*ibid*: 2), which I term "re-domaining," is crucial.

The concept of "assemblage" is homologous to that of "translation," emerging from the work of Deleuze and Guattari[5] (2004), and usually taken to refer to "complex becoming and multiple determinations ... sensitive to time and temporality in the emergence and mutation" of phenomena (Venn 2006: 107). The sense that assemblages involve "ensembles of heterogeneous elements" (Collier and Ong 2005: 5) which may or may not cohere in particular "regimes," but which should never be reified as "final or stable states" (Marcus and Saka 2006: 106), is a key part of the rendering of transnational or global processes as "problem-spaces" (Collier and Ong 2005: 14). As such, the concept not only questions the creation of ideal types of "welfare regimes," but also the idea of "path dependency" in welfare, much beloved by "historical institutionalist" theorists. Space precludes an examination of the diverse ways in which the various "institutionalisms" beloved of mainstream political science have impacted the study of social policy. As noted in Section III, I have even allowed myself to be seduced, at times, by such thinking. A useful overview (Broschek 2008) suggests that even in Pierson's (2004) conceptualization of historical institutionalism, small, contingent, and early events, which tend to create "lock-in" and "path-dependency" effects through positive feedback loops, can be broken by "exogenous shocks" which can create new "critical junctures." The problem, needless to say, here resides less in the processes described than in the conceptual apparatus and methodological reasoning.

Both Latour and Deleuze and Guattari focus less on "mundane states" and more on radical transformations, the struggle of new paradigms to emerge and, above all, on controversies that question the stability of "political," "technical," "scientific," "cultural" or "ethical" domains. Any phenomena which have a "distinctive capacity for ... abstractability and movement" (Collier and Ong 2005: 11) tend to produce equally distinct "lines of mutation" (*ibid*: 18) through the de- and re-articulation of elements. This suggests a strong preference for studying specific spatial-temporal moments or "conjunctures" produced by the coming together,

---

5 Most translations of Deleuze and Guattari translate the French word "*agencement*" as "assemblage." The authors rarely use the French word "*assemblage*," however (*cf.* Phillips, 2006, 108).

often in "perverse confluences" (Danigno 2007), of diverse trajectories, trends, pressures and forces (Clarke 2010). Too often, in critical social policy studies, there is an emphasis on what Williams (1977) termed "the epochal," reducing this complexity to the "rolling out" of a dominant tendency in which "the usual suspects," be they "globalization, neo-liberalism, modernity (or post-modernity), post-Fordism, or the needs/interests of capital" (Clarke 2004: 3) re-emerge endlessly to repeat the same scripts with the same conclusions.

As Lendvai and Bainton have recently suggested:

> Translation points to the danger of deciding, too early, that you know what something means, and of making decisions that provide closure to the research process. Such closures – whether theoretical or methodological – limit the possibilities of a continued dialogue across and between research sites, ideas, and participants. Where conceptual elaboration is understood to be the outcome of the research the focus shifts to understand "how" the research finds out as much as knowing "what" the research finds out (Lendvai and Bainton 2012).

At its most extensive, this cautions against attempting to develop "a truly global understanding of social welfare" (Midgely 2004: 217) which rests upon decontextualizing fundamentally contextualized (Northern and Western) concepts such as social welfare, social policy, and the welfare state. A double problem of translation emerges since concepts are, always, in more or less established relations with other concepts, embedded in linguistic forms which, in translation, can both lose and gain meanings and relations. In most Slavic languages, including Croatian, the concept of "welfare state" can be translated as "*socijalna država*" or "*država blagostanja*." Whilst the latter may be, literally, closer to the English, the former is widely accepted as the more accurate translation: indeed, Bauman, perhaps starting from the Polish language, tends to refer to "the social state" in his writings in English (Bauman 2005: 99). The complexities increase when we consider that "social" may be both "*socijalna*" and "*društvena*," the latter a more all-embracing concept of "societal" and the former rather too readily connoting a residual category (as a "social case"), whereas both "policy" and "politics" are "*politika*" in Croatian. Attempts to translate accurately "social policy," "social welfare," "social protection," "welfare capitalism," "social inclusion," and so on, are, of course, never solely questions of linguistics but involve a work of multiple translation, since the construction of new domains involves new forms, or chains, of conceptual linkages. The dominance of "policy English" or, even more so, of a new kind of "Euro-speak" in transnational reform encounters represents, for members and aspirant members of the European Union, a particular set of hegemonic resolutions of this difficulty.

Seeing social policy as a nested set of transnational processes working through practices of translation in multiple, emergent, and entangled assemblages, might offer new ways of understanding knowledge, power, and politics, bringing agency back in and re-asserting the importance of multi-sited ethnographic endeavors. Ethnographic methods contain within them a certain "capacity to surprise," described as the "aha effect" (Willis and Trondman 2000), providing certain privileged kinds of *entrées* into relationships and practices and their assemblage in translation. At the same time, of course, the ability to render knowledge across multiple sites, and the nature of flows across time and space, tends to be limited to that which the ethnographer observed, participated in, heard about, and/or speculated upon (Gould 2004). Whilst ethnographic methods are well suited to understanding how different forces, relationships and dynamics are condensed in particular locations, they are, perhaps, less useful in terms of articulating "the ways in which different sites, scales and spaces ... are articulated to one another" (Clarke and Stubbs 2010).

Social policy is always a multi-actored process, involving, at the very least, "policy elites, welfare providers, community service providers and welfare recipients" (Kingfisher 2011b), which struggle to be contained within linear narratives of "welfare regimes" and "policy transfer." The gap between research on "how policies reconfigure the lived realities of the people they affect" (Lendvai and Bainton 2011) and a classificatory literature on "regime typologies" is rather large, and not easily bridged. Elsewhere, I have drawn attention to the importance of diverse "intermediaries," active translators who are situated in complex power relations through their claims to "technical know-how" (Lendvai and Stubbs 2009b: 678). However, by focusing only on this level, the danger is of reifying complex social processes. At the same time, ideas of assemblages and translation offer a way into the production and reproduction of knowledge which allow certain agendas to emerge whilst others are actively silenced. The subject positions to which Kingfisher refers are, in themselves, complex constructions, simultaneously enabling and silencing, constraining and empowering, in highly selective, but always deeply conjunctural, ways. The "applied" nature of much social policy, of course, necessitates a critical reflexivity of the ways in which academic and research knowledge is often complicit in these constructions. This is crucial in understanding dominant forms of research on social policy in so-called Eastern Europe.

3. Re-domaining the social in the "new" Eastern Europe: Hybridities and contestations

Eastern Europe was "invented" or, more specifically, "re-invented" in the years between 1989 and 1991, as diverse geo-political, popular, journalistic, intellectual, and international agency practices all converged to construct the idea of a "new" region undergoing a "post-communist transition," to be judged according to a "norm" of "Western Europe," much as in its original invention in the 19th century (Wolff 1994). The fact that, in many cases, this transition coincided with new nation-state building, in the break-up of the former Soviet Union, former Yugoslavia, and former Czechoslovakia, and the re-unification of Germany further contributed to the rush to describe, label, and prescribe. The wars of the Yugoslav succession and other conflicts in the successor states of the Soviet Union introduced a conflict and post-conflict dynamic, adding to the range of discourses and agency agendas in play. In short, the opening up of a "new" frontier for the expansion of capitalist economic systems in the context of the discovery of so-called "democratic deficits"; the fact that some of the newly created countries were, or quickly became, extremely poor; and the dramatic consequences of wars, killings, and mass forced migration in or "on the edge of" Europe generated intense interest in a "great transformation" far beyond that described by Polanyi (Polanyi 2001). Like the previous "great transformation" this, too, involved the planned introduction of free markets. Of course, unlike nineteenth-century England, the region played host to a whole army of outside advisors, consultants, and organizations claiming knowledge, carrying prescriptions, and asserting the right to intervene in this planning.

The need to understand the causes and consequences of these transformations also led to an explosion of "transitology" literature, previously a rather marginal political science tradition exploring change in Southern Europe, in particular post-authoritarian Spain and Portugal, and Latin America. The approach, whether in crude or more sophisticated forms, suggested that transformations in the "new" Eastern Europe were part of a global modernization process in which rational actors would introduce the fundamentals of liberal democracy: the rule of law, political pluralist competition, free markets, and an autonomous sphere of civil society. As a corollary of this, any factors hindering this process, be they ethnicized, cultural, religious, and/or linguistic identifications, were seen as anti-modern and parochial, to be swept away or rendered irrelevant by powerful transnational forces and processes (Tokes 2000). It is certainly the case that the "first wave" of advice and reform, commonly known as "shock therapy," either ignored the social dimension completely, endangered social protection systems through drastic reductions in social expenditures, or otherwise delinked the "social" from the core agenda of political and economic reforms (Murrell 1993; Wedel 1999).

At the same time, the ways in which "progressive" global agencies, notably UNICEF through its TransMONEE project, which has produced regional monitoring reports and a database covering, by now, 28 post-communist countries in

Eastern Europe[6], and, to a lesser extent, UNDP through its Human Development Reports,[7] sought to draw attention to the social costs of transition, and to suggest the need for more comprehensive social protection systems, reinforced precisely the dominant logic of a "region in transition" and, indeed, the broad logic of transitology. UNICEF's 1994 report, based on only 9 countries because data from many countries in the region was missing, incomplete, or inaccurate, suggested that "the mortality and health crisis burdening most Eastern European countries since 1989 is without precedent in the European peacetime history of this century … (and signals) a societal crisis of unexpected proportions, unknown implications and uncertain solutions" (UNICEF 1994: vi). The next report, extending the data set to 18 countries, noted "a severe welfare crisis affecting especially children and adolescents, an upsurge in mortality, equally shocking falls in births and increases in poverty, and falling social protection and child development programmes" (UNICEF 1995: v). These "facts" shaped the response in terms of the need for a "re-domained" social and greater emphasis on social protection "safety nets" (*cf.* Standing 1996). In this way, the report also led to an analysis of the causes of failure to develop more comprehensive social protection systems, and to complete agreement regarding the right and necessity to intervene.

Crucially, these interventions created certain "technologies of understanding" through which the increasing divergence of outcomes in terms of well-being over time and the uneven pace of economic and political reforms, judged according to Northern and Western constructions and indices, of course, led to speculation on the diverse drivers and blockages of change, and to a new growth industry labelling the varieties of capitalism and welfare regimes in the new Eastern Europe. Authors rushed to label and classify, in many cases with little or no direct knowledge of many of the countries and territories in their studies. My own work for UNDP (UNDP 2011) and for UNICEF, particularly a recent collaboration with Alfio Cerami (Cerami and Stubbs 2011), precisely fits into this body of work. At a broad, structural level, there may be value in linking, as we did, the nature and sources of growth (which may be export-led, oil-based, remittance or development assistance based), the nature of the crisis, and patterns of welfare provision, especially when political agency in terms of types of "elite capture" are brought back into the picture (*cf.* Stubbs and Zrinščak 2011 on "clientelism"). The argument that those states which have more developed social protection systems are more resistant to crisis, and appear to recover more quickly as social protection

6 http://www.transmonee.org/ (accessed 12 March 2012). The first report was in 1993.
7 http://hdr.undp.org/en/ (accessed 12 March 2012). The first HDR was issued in 1990.

forms a key "institutional complementarity" (Hall and Soskice (eds) 2001), may also have some merit, and may even have leverage on policy makers told to adhere to "evidence-based" social policies. At the same time, the creation of a crude continuum of types from "state-enabled" through "state-influenced" and then "state-interfered" market economies (Cerami and Stubbs 2011) not only emits judgements on the basis of a biased, Western lens, but also comes very close to reinforcing a new "neo-liberal" orthodoxy regarding the role of the state.

The inevitable problems of what has been called "welfare modeling business" (Abrahamson 1999), but is more akin to a "welfare labeling business," reaches its apotheosis in discussions about the 28 post-communist countries of the imagined "New" Eastern Europe. Notwithstanding a common starting point in the transitology models, these labels, whether of a smaller sub-set of countries, or through the elaboration of sub-regional or other clusters within the region as a whole, vary greatly and capture far too little of the dynamic and uneven processes of emerging welfare assemblages. My recent review, with Alfio Cerami, of the many and varied labels[8] suggests they "highlight only particular characteristics of

8 "Shkaratan (2007) and Hanson and Teague (2007) defin(e) the Russian Federation as a new form of 'etacratism' or of 'political capitalism' whereas Lane (2008), emphasizing political co-ordination, labeled it as 'state influenced capitalism.' Mykhnenko (2007) has described Ukraine as "social market regulated capitalism', while Charman (2007) has defined Kazakhstan as a 'state-led liberalized market economy'. Other more general classifications have also included Hancké, Rhodes, and Thatcher's (2007) definition of post-communist capitalisms as 'emerging market economies' (EMEs), Nölke and Vliegenthart's (2009) definition of 'dependent market economies' or Tridico's (2011) definition of 'state capitalism' for Turkmenistan, Belarus, and Uzbekistan, 'hybrid capitalism' for Romania, Bulgaria, Bosnia Herzegovina, and Ukraine, 'dirigiste capitalism' for Azerbaijan, Kyrgyzstan, Serbia, Moldova, Russia, Tajikistan and Montenegro, 'corporative capitalism' for the Czech Republic, Croatia, Hungary, Macedonia Poland, and Slovenia, and 'competitive capitalism' (with some dirigiste and corporatist tendencies) for Albania, Armenia, Georgia, Estonia, Kazakhstan, Latvia, Lithuania, and the Slovak Republic. The recent and highly influential work of Bohle and Greskovits (2007) has divided the Central and Eastern European region into three substantially different sub-clusters, depending on the degree of convergence on a neo-liberal model. These correspond to a 'neo-liberal' type in the Baltic states, an 'embedded neo-liberal' type in the Visegrad states, and a 'neo-corporatist' type in Slovenia (see also Lendvai, 2009). In terms of Central and Eastern Europe, Deacon (1992) described Poland as a '*post-communist conservative corporatist*' welfare state, Czechoslovakia as a 'social democratic' model, while Hungary was seen as a 'liberal welfare regime' (see also Ferge, 2001). For Aidukaite (2006, 2010), Cerami (2006) and Żukowski (2009), the ten new Eastern EU member states can be described in terms of

a more variegated pattern of political and economic decision-making" (Cerami and Stubbs 2011: 12). Indeed, in this context it is interesting to note how the concept of a "hybrid" welfare regime has migrated from a more post-structuralist literature into the mainstream of the literature on types of "welfare regimes" and forms of "welfare capitalism."

Noting that "(t)he comparative act is… not a rational choice based on initial analyses of similarities and difference (but) …is a political act that creates certain associations and allows for certain meanings at the expense of others," Lendvai and Bainton (2011) go on to suggest that most comparisons compare emerging Eastern European welfare regimes with each other and, above all, with those of Western Europe. A rare exception is Haggard and Kauffman's book (2008) where the comparators are Latin America and East Asia. They present Eastern Europe as characterized by "comprehensive," if not "universal," social protection coverage, and "limited liberalization." This is, in fact, a rather simplistic picture, failing to capture the heterogeneous nature of welfare settlements in Eastern Europe (cf. Bohle and Greskovits 2007; Brust and Greskovits 2009; Lendvai 2011). The flaw in all of this, of course, is not just the choice of comparator and the time period under discussion, but the rather crude input-output understanding of what social policy and social welfare are, and the suggestion that, on the basis of a number of variables, clear regime types have already emerged. If, as appears to be the case, "hybridity," complexity, and contradiction are so prevalent, the need for a different kind of research is clearly indicated.

A related literature emerged which charted the influence of international, transnational, and global actors on social welfare and its reform in the "new" Eastern Europe, suggesting that a view of these actors as all-powerful and transferring a "one size fits all," essentially "neo-liberal," model of social policy could not be sustained in the context of key debates within and between international organizations and, crucially, in interactions with so-called "domestic" actors. Nevertheless, research on the role of the World Bank in promoting a model of "radical," three-pillar pension reforms throughout "the region" in the late 1990s

---

a distinct post-communist welfare regime type, while for Szalai (2005), Gans-Morse and Orenstein (2006), and Fuchs and Offe (2009), a mixture of corporatism and liberalism or of corporatism and social democracy (Fenger, 2007) is the main characteristic of these countries. Other more diversified categorizations also exist. For Szikra (2004), Tomka (2004), Bakken (2008), *Sirovátka and Saxonberg* (2008), and Hacker (2009), a hybrid mix of *neo-liberalism*, *corporatism* and *social democracy* is a key feature in this region, which crystallizes in a variety of different and not easy to identify forms" (Cerami and Stubbs, 2011; 11).

did point to the way in which the formation of a strong epistemic community, including key pension reform figures from Latin America in the 1980s, had a strong influence, reflecting global trends towards individualization, privatization, and marketization (Muller 2002; Orenstein 2005). As has been more broadly argued, "the legitimacy and credibility of the (World) Bank's expertise is drawn through a circular process between the knowledge it produces and the audiences that legitimize that knowledge" (St Clair 2006: 77). At the same time, the need to "translate" policy prescriptions into specific national contexts, and in a crowded space of a multiplicity of agencies and prescriptions, with dominant prescriptions changing over time, suggests the need for closer ethnographic analyses of the reforms (*cf.* Stubbs and Zrinščak 2007). Still, most studies tell us little about the processes involved and, in any case, pension reforms cannot automatically be assumed to indicate the nature of change in other social policy spheres.

The emergence of the European Union as a more significant actor, at least for those "post-communist" countries aspiring to EU membership, eight of whom joined in May 2004, with Bulgaria and Romania joining in January 2007, led to a new literature on the impacts of processes of "Europeanization." Whilst much of this work tended to address the institutional conditionalities of EU accession, a kind of interpretative turn was taken by those scholars building on the experience of previous EU enlargements, notably those of post-authoritarian Spain, Portugal, and Greece, regarding the idea of "cognitive Europeanization." This refers to "soft" socialization and learning processes through which policy makers, in the context of new actor mobilizations, come to "re-domain" social policy concerns in terms of "social inclusion," "anti-discrimination," "work-life balance," and so on (Radaelli 2000; Guillen and Alvarez 2004; Sotiropolous 2004). Authors of studies at this time (prior to, and immediately consequent upon, accession) tended to see the content of social policy as still following residual and neo-liberal patterns, while EU influence was more detectable in the processes and procedures of policy making through the "Open Method of Co-ordination" akin to a process of benchmarking and shared learning against agreed objectives (Ferge 2001; Ferge and Juhasz 2004; Potucek 2004; Guillen and Palier 2004; Ferrera 2005).

A key distinction can be made between "strategies for 'transition'" and "actually existing 'transition', the actual processes and dynamics of change" (Fairclough 2005: 1). Fairclough links transition in the "new" Eastern Europe with the proliferation of "re-scaling" strategies, in which multiple narratives struggle for dominance in the process of "recontextualization" and "operationalization." Looking at the transposing of the EU strategic focus on "poverty and social exclusion" into Romanian social policy and practice, he points both to the "colonizing" effects of this and to the complex ways in which the strategy "necessarily enters the internal field of strategic positions and strategic struggles, where it can be appropriated in diverse ways with diverse outcomes" (*ibid*: 18). His focus is on "how and under what conditions discourses are *enacted* as new ways of acting and interacting and new social relationships, *inculcated* as new ways of being, new identities, and *materialized* … in new ways of organizing time and space in institutions and organizations" (*ibid*: 6). Lendvai's (2007) careful steering between "institutionalist" and more "critical" scholarship, also sees "Europeanization" more in terms of an "encounter," as a kind of "double movement" of "embedding" between "the European" and "the national," involving multiple and contested constructions of subjectivities, identities, and "new" policy domains. National social policy frameworks become, in her terms, "reframed," sometimes in paradoxical forms in different policy domains, including "active inclusion," "employment," "anti discrimination," "gender equality," as well as "social protection," including "pensions, health and long-term care," and "social inclusion." As we argue elsewhere, there is nothing "natural" or easily translatable about any of these domaining concepts (Lendvai and Stubbs 2007). Seeing the social dimension of the EU as "an assemblage of innovative policy ideas" (Lendvai 2007: 32) presents a challenge for researchers to, precisely, "unfold the subtle processes of transformation of social policy meanings, discourses, ideas, policy tools and objectives" (*ibid*: 32).

My work with Noémi Lendvai, particularly that which explores social policies in Southeastern Europe as a set of contested spaces of governance, nation-state-building, and indeed of citizenship at the intersection of discourses of "Europeanization" and of "development," tries to enter the "black box" of reform processes where social policy remains profoundly unsettled and complexly articulated in the context of discourses of, *inter alia*, "security," "migration," "refugee return," "human rights," and "cross-border" claims and entitlements (*cf.* Lendvai and Stubbs 2009b). We show how, in different places at different times, a large number of diverse policy translators and project intermediaries operate in flexible and fluid spaces, blurring the borders between "technocratic" and "political" interactions, and often relying on "personal authority." Whilst the multiplication and fragmentation of interventions often leads to prescriptions which are "unfit to fit," the ways in which certain actors and positions are strengthened whilst others are marginalized, whether it be through the mediating framework of "new public management" and/or the construction of key "coalitions for change," are vital in terms of where social policy fits in relation to a privileged "economic" discourse and which policies and practices tend to be enacted, albeit in translation and as a part of complex assemblages. Revisiting some of my consultancy experiences working on reform projects and programs, it is clear that the improvisational nature of many of the "logics in translation," with encounters often resembling "contact zones" in which radical asymmetries of power lead to profound differences in understanding of key terms and processes, does not mean that "nothing is done," but rather reframes reforms beyond a supposed technical logic (Stubbs 2011). Currently, in the context of work with the European Commission, I see how "soft" governance in social policy is translated to policy makers and key intermediaries in the new candidate countries, with Commission officials, for example after a recent seminar in Montenegro, suggesting that the Ministry presentations "reminded us of Croatia when we started the process there."

The impact of the waves of economic and financial crises on social policy in the European Union and beyond is still largely un-researched, except in broad brush stroke terms. It is clear that responses to the crisis have re-animated a crowded transnational space, re-inhabited by the international financial institutions, primarily the World Bank and, even more importantly, the International Monetary Fund. Notwithstanding the many contradictions in their role, this re-emergence, in a new and complex partnership with the European Union, as managers of the crisis and legitimators of emergent transnational assemblages is of immense importance. The re-emergence of the crisis within the Eurozone and, in particular, reactions to the potential of a Greek debt default, have, at least for the moment, reconfigured the relationship between "economic" and "social policies," with new forms of austerity packages being presented, regardless of political fall-out, in a number of countries. How the EU works in partnership with the IFIs in these contexts is a subject of speculation rather than empirical research. Crucially, the crisis occurs alongside a revision of the European Union's strategic focus, with the Europe 2020 initiative linking "smart," "sustainable," and "inclusive" growth and setting, for the first time, an ambitious target of lifting 20 million people in the European Union out of poverty and social exclusion.

A new wave of structural reforms has emerged involving a recalibration of economic, fiscal, and welfare policies (Lendvai 2009) and a reframing of social welfare in the context of a discourse about public finance and indebtedness. Under Europe 2020, at the moment at least, the Open Method of Co-ordination appears to have been seriously weakened as a catalyst for a re-domained "social" in some of the "new" member states. At the same time, the nature of the crisis in some so-called "peripheral" "old" member states may lead to a reconfiguring of the EU's social dimension as a whole. Whilst processes and practices in terms of "social inclusion" generate new claims on public expenditures and identify new needs, this is challenged by effective capping of social expenditures, a disciplinarity in terms of tight fiscal policies, and a reform agenda in terms of institutional "capacity building" (Lendvai 2009). It is this paradox and set of contradictory practices which needs to be managed, in part at least, through new "meta-critical partnerships" between the IMF and the European Union (Lendvai and Stubbs 2010). The crisis confirms, in effect, the need for conducting rigorous conjunctural analysis, combined with thick ethnographic descriptions of the varied attempts at "crisis management," rather than addressing it only in terms of broad and sweeping generalizations.

How these discourses and practices impact on the ground, at the interface between public welfare officials and their clients, has hardly been researched in the "new" Eastern Europe. Haney's study in Hungary addressed the frustrations of (women) welfare workers unable to meet the needs of their (desperate) clients in "a crumbling welfare state that was replete with pain and dislocation" (Haney 2000: 48). The ways in which frontline staff merged "global discourses of need" with more local discourses of "pathology" to construct a model of "undeserving clients" is relevant in the context of the increasing attention paid, at least on a discursive level, to conditionalities to be imposed on that section of the poor "capable of work." The tensions between hard stretched public welfare services and new service-oriented and/or advocacy driven non-governmental organizations skilled in bidding for and implementing a range of experimental or "pilot" projects is also important (*cf.* Maglajlić and Stubbs 2012; Maglajlić Holiček and Rašidagić 2007). The lack of work on the ways in which service users may or may not fit into models of "ideal clients," "deserving of support" through "individual needs" or "membership" of "vulnerable groups," is a major lacuna in research. The need to combine ethnographies with "ethnohistories" (Haney *ibid.*), exploring the complex relationship, over time, between welfare, work, nation, citizenship, and gender (tying eligibility to motherhood), has barely been addressed in the "new" Eastern Europe.

4. Conclusion: For an "ethics of translation" in research, policy, and practice

In this and in other works, I have attempted to develop a vocabulary, epistemology, and methodology which emphasizes "the interactions, the complexity, and the liminality of encounters between actors, sites, scales and contexts" (Lendvai and Stubbs 2009a: 224). The concepts of policy translation and assemblages capture well the ways in which policy meanings are being constantly transformed, translated, distorted, and modified. Methodologically, this has involved a search for "reflexive spaces," privileging the "periphery" over the supposed "center" to chart various forms of "displacement," "disciplining," and "depoliticization" in social relations, in the process taking a "post-colonial turn" not merely as "an object of desire for critical practice" (Slemon 1995: 45), but as an entry point for a clearer understanding of "the operation of power, domination, the formation of hegemonic practices and the technologies of maintaining relations of dependency and control" (Lendvai and Stubbs 2009a: 226). The use of "case vignettes," based on a "bending and blending" (Lendvai and Stubbs 2007: 183) of roles, including that of researcher, has offered an *entrée* into the study of social policy as "a constant move between the formal and the informal, the institutionalized and unofficial practices, the paperwork and 'the reality'" (*ibid.*). At the same time, the confusion which arises from occupying a series of liminal research spaces while also contributing to policy planning and engaging in political advocacy cannot be denied.

Having earlier dismissed much of what counts as "comparative social policy," there is a clear need for theoretically-informed, multi-sited, ethnographic, and social-scientific collaborations. Researchers familiar with "welfare" in different parts of the world might come together in ways which necessarily privilege the importance of "translation" devices within a kind of "meta-ethnography," rescuing the concept from its origins in mainly clinical health care research (Noblit and Hare 1988). How we are to "imbue the concept of translation with an ethical force" (Strathern 2011), so that included within a policy are conceptions and practices that deal with "how it might get translated for any specific location" (*ibid.*), is a key challenge facing critical ethnographers of welfare insofar as they still want to "make a difference." Lendvai and Bainton's (2011) discussion of this in terms of de Sousa Santos' idea of a sociology of "emergences" to address concrete possibilities and capacities (Santos 2004), with due regard to Amartya Sen's concern with functionings and capabilities (Sen 1999) as refracted through a Freireian lens of "conscientization" (Freire 1996), may allow for new forms of "vocality" (Ferrera, 2005; 179) or "talking back" (Lendvai and Bainton 2011) to emerge. In the end, the challenge is to maximize the possibilities contained in the sense that "reflexive translation has the capacity to do more than make us sensitive to the politics of policy transfer," in terms of offering "new critical possibilities of social change" (*ibid.*).

References

Abrahamson, Peter. 1999. "The Welfare Modelling Business." *Social Policy and Administration,* Vol. 33, No. 4. 394–415.

Aidukaite, Jolanta. 2010. "Welfare Reforms in Central and Eastern Europe: A New Type of Welfare Regime?" *Ekonomika,* Vol. 89, No. 4. 7–24.

Aidukaite, Jolanta. 2006. "The Formation of Social Insurance Institutions of the Baltic States in the Post Socialist Era." *Journal of European Social Policy*, Vol. 16, No. 3. 259–270.

Bakken, Geoffrey. 2008. "Social Protection Systems in Central and Eastern Europe: A New "World of Welfare"?" Masters' Thesis, Wisconsin-Madison: University of Wisconsin-Madison.

Bauman, Zygmunt. 2005. *Work, Consumerism and the New Poor*. Milton Keynes: Open University Press.

Bohle, Dorothee, and Bela Greskovits. 2007. "Neoliberalism, Embedded Neoliberalism, and Neocorporatism: Paths Towards Transnational Capitalism in Central-Eastern Europe." *West European Politics*, Vol. 30, No. 3. 443–466.

Broschek, Jorg. 2008. "Historical Institutionalism and Canadian Social Policy: assessing two models of policy change" Paper for workshop of the Canadian Political Science Association, http://www.cpsa-acsp.ca/papers-2008/Broschek.pdf. Accessed March 7, 2012.

Bruszt, Laszlo, and Bela Greskovits. 2009. "Transnationalization, Social Integration, and Capitalist Diversity in the East and the South" *Studies in Comparative International Development*, Vol. 44. 411–4.

Callon, Michel. 1986. "Some elements of a sociology of translation: domestication of the scallops and the fishermen of St. Brieuc Bay" In *Power, Action and Belief – a new sociology of knowledge?*, edited by John Law, Sociological Review Monograph 34, London: Routledge, 196–234.

Cerami, Alfio. 2006. *Social Policy in Central and Eastern Europe: The Emergence of a New European Welfare Regime*. Berlin: LIT Verlag.

Cerami, Alfio, and Paul Stubbs. 2011. "Post-Communist Welfare Capitalisms: bringing institutions and agency back in", Institute of Economics, Zagreb, Working Paper 11/03.

Chamberlayne, Prue, Cooper, Andrew, Freeman, Richard, and Michael Rustin (eds.) 1999. *Welfare and Culture in Europe: towards a new paradigm in social policy*. London: Jessica Kingsley.

Charman, Ken. 2007. "Kazakhstan: A State Led Liberalized Market Economy?" In *Varieties of Capitalism in Post-Communist Countries*, edited by David Lane and Martin Myant. Basingstoke: Palgrave Macmillan, 165–182.

Clarke, John. 2004. *Changing Welfare, Changing States: new directions in social policy*. London: Sage.

Clarke, John. 2010. "Of crises and conjunctures: the problem of the present." *Journal of Communication Inquiry*, Vol. 34, No. 4. 337–354.

Clarke, John, and Paul Stubbs. 2011. "Making Policy Move: the challenge of tracing transnational translation" Paper to conference 'Beyond Esssentialisms', Ljubljana, November, 2011.

Clifford, James. 1997. *Routes: travel and translation in the late twentieth century.* Cambridge, MA: Harvard University.

Collier, Stephen, and Aihwa Ong. 2005. "Global Assemblages, Anthropological Problems" In *Global Assemblages: technology, politics, and ethics as anthropological problems*, edited by Aihwa Ong and Stephen Collier. Oxford: Blackwell, 3–21.

Dagnino, Evalina. 2007. "Citizenship: a perverse confluence." *Development in Practice,* Vol. 17, No. 4/5.

Deacon, Bob. 1992. *The New Eastern Europe: Social Policy, Past, Present and Future.* London: Sage.

Deacon, Bob, Hulse, Michelle, and Paul Stubbs. 1997. *Global Social Policy: international organizations and the future of welfare*. London: Sage.

Deleuze, Jacques, and Felix Guattari. 2004. *A Thousand Plateaus*. London: Continuum, first English edition, 1987.

Fairclough, Norman. 2005. "Critical discourse analysis in trans-disciplinary research on social change: transition, re-scaling, poverty and social inclusion." *Lodz Papers in Pragmatics,* Vol. 1. 37–58.

Fenger, Menno. 2007. "Welfare regimes in Central and Eastern Europe: Incorporating Post-Communist Countries in a Welfare Regime Typology." *Contemporary Issues and Ideas in Social Sciences,* Vol. 3, No. 2. 1–30.

Ferge, Zsuzsa. 2001. "European Integration and the Reform of Social Security in the Accession Countries." *Journal of European Social Quality,* Vol. 3, No. 1–2. 9–25.

Ferge, Zsuzsa, and Gabor Juhasz. 2004. "Accession and Social Policy: the case of Hungary." *Journal of European Social Policy,* Vol. 14, No. 3. 233–251.

Ferrera, Maurizio. 2005. *The Boundaries of Welfare: European integration and the new spatial politics of social protection.* Oxford: Oxford University Press.

Freeman, Richard. 2009. "What is 'translation'?" *Evidence and Policy,* Vol. 5, No. 4. 429–547.

Freire, Paolo. 1996. *Pedagogy of the Oppressed.* London: Penguin.

Fuchs, Susanne, and Claus Offe. 2009. "Welfare State Formation in the Enlarged European Union: Patterns of Reform in the Post-Communist New Member States." In *The SAGE Handbook of European Studies,* edited by Chris Rumford. London: Sage, 420–441.

Gans-Morse, Jordan, and Mitchell A. Orenstein. 2006. "Postcommunist Welfare States: The Emergence of a Continental-Liberal World" Paper presented at the 38th National Convention of the American Association for the Advancement of Slavic Studies, Washington D.C., November 16–19, 2006.

Gould, Jeremy. 2004. "Positionality and scale: methodological issues in the ethnography of aid." In *Ethnographies of Aid: exploring development texts encounters*, edited by Jeremy Gould and Henrik Secher Marcussen. IDS Occasional paper 24, Roskilde University, Denmark, 263–290.

Guillen, Ana, and Santiago Alvarez. 2004. "The EU's Impact on the Spanish Welfare State: the role of cognitive Europeanization." *Journal of European Social Policy,* Vol. 14, No. 3. 285–299.

Guillen, Ana, and Bruno Palier. 2004. "Introduction: does Europe matter? Accession to the EU and social policy developments in recent and new member states." *Journal of European Social Policy,* Vol. 14, No. 3. 203–209.

Hacker, Bjorn. 2009. "Hybridization instead of Clustering: Transformation Processes of Welfare Policies in Central and Eastern Europe." *Social Policy & Administration,* Vol. 43, No. 2. 52–169.

Haggard, Stephen, and Robert Kauffman. 2008. *Development, Democracy and Welfare States*. Princeton: University Press.

Hall, Peter, and David Soskice (eds.) 2001. *Varieties of Capitalism: the institutional foundations of comparative advantage*. Oxford: Oxford University Press.

Hancké, Bob, Rhodes, Martin, and Mark Thatcher (eds.) 2007. *Beyond Varieties of Capitalism. Conflict, Contradictions, and Complementarities in the European Economy.* Oxford: Oxford University Press.

Haney, Lynne. 2000. "Global Discourses of Need: mythologizing and pathologizing welfare in Hungary." In *Global Ethnography: forces, connections and imaginings in a postmodern world,* edited by Michael Burawoy et al. Berkeley: University of California Press, 48–73.

Hanson, Phillip, and Elizabeth Teague. 2007. "Russian Political Capitalism and its Environment," In *Varieties of Capitalism in Post-Communist Countries,* edited by David Lane and Martin Myant. Basingstoke: Palgrave Macmillan, 149–164.

Jambresić Kirin, Renata, and Maja Povrzanović (eds.). 1996. *War, Exile, Everyday Life: cultural perspectives*. Zagreb: IEF.

Kingfisher, Catherine. 2011a "Tracing Policy: translation and assemblage," Panel Abstract for American Anthropological Association Annual Conference, Montreal, December.

Kingfisher, Catherine. 2011b. "Assembling Convergence and Divergence: Policy transfer and everyday policy knowledge in Aotearoa/New Zealand and Alberta, Canada." Paper presented to American Anthropological Association Annual Conference, Montreal, December, 2011.

Lane, David. 2008. "From Chaotic to State-Led Capitalism." *New Political Economy*, Vol. 13, No. 2. 177–184.

Latour, Bruno. 1987. "The power of association." In *Power, Action and Belief – a new sociology of knowledge?*, edited by John Law, Sociological Review Monograph 34. London: Routledge, 262–280.

Lendvai, Noemi. 2004. "The weakest link? EU Accession: Dialoguing EU and post-communist social policy." *Journal of European Social Policy*, Vol. 14, No. 3. 319–333.

Lendvai, Noemi. 2007. "Europeanization of social policy? Prospects and challenges for South East Europe." In *Social Policy and International Interventions in South East Europe*, edited by Bob Deacon and Paul Stubbs. Edward Elgar: Cheltenham, 22–44.

Lendvai, Noemi. 2009. "Varieties of Post-Communist Welfare: Europeanisation and emerging welfare regimes in the new EU member states," Paper presented to RC 19 meeting in Montreal, web: http://www.cccg.umontreal.ca/RC19/PDF/Lendvai-N_Rc192009.pdf. Accessed March 13, 2012.

Lendvai, Noemi. 2011. "EU Integration and Post-communist Welfare: Catch-up convergence before and after the economic crisis." In *Convergence in the Enlarged EU*, edited by Eren Ipek. Farnham: Ashgate.

Lendvai, Noemi, and David Bainton. 2011. "Unfit to fit? Ruptures and erasures in the translation of the global Education for All agenda in Tibetan communities of Ladakh, India." American Anthropological Association, Montreal, December.

Lendvai, Noemi, and David Bainton. 2012. "Translation: Towards a Critical Comparative Social Policy Agenda." In *Handbook of Comparative Social Policy*, edited by Patricia Kennett, new edition. Cheltenham: Edward Elgar. Forthcoming.

Lendvai, Noemi, and Paul Stubbs. 2007. "Policies as Translation: situating transnational social policies." In *Policy Reconsidered: meanings, politics and practices*, edited by Sue Hodgson and Zoe Irving. Policy Press: Bristol, 173–189.

Lendvai, Noemi, and Paul Stubbs. 2009a. "*Globale Sozialpolitik und Governance: Standpunkte, Politik und Postkolonialismus* (Global Social Policy and Governance: positionality, politics and post-colonialism)" In *Nord-Süd Beziehungen im Umbruch: Neu Perpektiven auf Staat und Demokratie in der Weltpolitik,* edited by Hans-Jürgen Burchardt. Frankfurt: Campus Verlag, 219–244.

Lendvai, Noemi, and Paul Stubbs. 2009b. "Assemblages, Translation, and Intermediaries in South East Europe: rethinking transnationalism and social policy." *European Societies,* Vol. 11 No. 5. 673–695.

Lendvai, Noemi, and Paul Stubbs. 2010. "Translation, Social Policy and the Crisis: revisiting post-structuralist theories in Central and Eastern Europe." Paper for RC 19 Session, World Congress of Sociology, Gothenburg July, 2010.

Maglajlić, Reima Ana, and Paul Stubbs. 2012. "The Transnational Politics of Social Work in Post-Conflict and Transition Contexts: reflections from South East Europe." *British Journal of Social Work,* forthcoming.

Maglajlić Holiček, Reima Ana, and Ešref Kenan Rašidagić. 2007. "Bosnia and Herzegovina." In *Social Policy and International Interventions in South East Europe,* edited by Bob Deacon and Paul Stubbs. Cheltenham: Edward Elgar, 149–166.

Marcus, George, and Erhan Saka. 2006. "Assemblage." *Theory, Culture, Society,* Vol. 23 No. 2/3. 101–106.

Midgely, James. 2004. "Social development and social welfare: implications for social policy." In *A Handbook of Comparative Social Policy,* edited by Patricia Kennett. Cheltenham: Edward Elgar, 217–238.

Müller, Katharina. 2002. "From the state to the market? Pension reform paths in central-Eastern Europe and the former Soviet Union." *Social Policy and Administration,* Vol. 36 No. 2. 156–175.

Murrell, Peter. 1993. "What is Shock Therapy? What Did it Do in Poland and Russia?" *Post-Soviet Affairs* 9.2. 111–40.

Mykhnenko, Vlada. 2007. "Strengths and Weaknesses of 'Weak' Coordination: Economic Institutions, Revealed Comparative Advantages, and Socio-Economic Performance of Mixed Market Economies in Poland and Ukraine." In *Beyond Varieties of Capitalism: Conflict, Contradictions, and Complementarities in the European Economy,* edited by Bob Hancké, Martin Rhodes and Mark Thatcher. Oxford: Oxford University Press, 351–378.

Newton, Tim. 1996. "Agency and Discourse: recruiting consultants in a life insurance company." *Sociology,* Vol. 30, No. 4. 717–739.

Noblit, George, and R. Dwight Hare. 1988. *Meta-ethnography: synthesising qualitative studies.* Qualitative Research Methods, Volume 11. London: Sage.

Nölke, Andreas, and Arjan Vliegenthart. 2009. "Enlarging the Varieties of Capitalism: the Emergence of Dependent Market Economies in East Central Europe." *World Politics,* Vol. 61 No. 4. 670–702.

Orenstein, Mitchell. 2005. "The new pension reform as global policy." *Global Social Policy*, Vol. 5 No. 2. 175–202.

Phillips, John. 2006. "*Agencement*/Assemblage." *Theory, Culture, Society* Vol. 23, No. 2/3. 108–110.

Pierson, Paul. 2004. *Politics in Time: history, institutions and social analysis.* Princeton: University Press.

Polanyi, Karl. 2001. *The Great Transformation: the political and economic origins of our time.* New York: Beacon Press, first published 1944.

Potucek, Martin. 2004. "Accession and Social Policy: the case of the Czech Republic." *Journal of European Social Policy* Vol. 14, No. 3. 233–266.

Radaelli, Claudio. 2000. "Whither Europeanization? Conceptual stretching and substantive change." *European Integration Online Papers* 4(8), http://eiop.or.at/eiop/pdf/2000-008.pdf. Accessed March 13, 2012.

St. Clair, Asuncion. 2006. "Global Poverty: the co-production of knowledge and politics." *Global Social Policy* 6.1. 57–77.

Sakai, Naoki. 2006. "Translation." *Theory, Culture, Society* Vol. 23, No. 2/3. 71–78.

Sousa Santos, Boaventura de. 2004. *The World Social Forum: a users' manual.* http://www.ces.uc.pt/bss/documentos/fsm_eng.pdf. Accessed March 13, 2012.

Sen, Amartya. 1999. *Development as Freedom.* Oxford: University Press.

Shkaratan, Ovsey. 2007. "The Russian Transformation: A New Form of Etacratism?" In *The Transformation of State Socialism: System Change, Capitalism or Something Else?*, edited by David Lane. Basingstoke: Palgrave Macmillan, 143–158.

Shore, Chris, and Susan Wright (eds.). 1997. *Anthropology of Policy: critical perspectives on governance and power.* London: Routledge.

Shore, Chris, and Susan Wright. 2011. "Conceptualising Policy: Technologies of Governance and the Politics of Visibility." In *Policy Worlds: anthropology and the analysis of contemporary power*, edited by Chris Shore, Susan Wright and David Peró. Oxford: Berghahn, 1–25.

Sirovátka, Tomas, and Stephen Saxonberg. 2008. "Neo-liberalism by Decay? The Evolution of the Czech Welfare State," Paper presented at the Annual ESPAnet Conference, Helsinki, September 18–20, 2008.

Slemon, Stephen 1995. "The Scramble for Post Colonialism." In *The Post-Colonial Studies Reader*, edited by Bill Ashcroft, Gareth Griffiths and Helen Tiffin. London: Routledge, 45–85.

Sotiropolous, Dimitri. 2004. "The EU's Impact on the Greek Welfare State: Europeanization on paper." *Journal of European Social Policy* 14. 3. 267–284.

Standing, Guy. 1996. "Social protection in central and eastern Europe: A tale of slipping anchors and torn safety nets?" In *Welfare States in Transition: National Adaptations in Global Economies, edited by Gosta Esping-Anderson.* London: Sage for UNRISD, 225–255.

Strathern, Marilyn. 2011. Discussant's Comments, AAA Conference, Montreal.

Stubbs, Paul. 2002. "Globalisation, memory and welfare regimes in transition: towards an anthropology of transnational policy transfers" *International Journal of Social Welfare* Vol. 11 No. 4. 321–330.

Stubbs, Paul. 2011. "'Managing' *Consultancy*: Charisma, Competence and Translation in Transnational Spaces." Paper for AAA Annual Conference, Montreal, 2011.

Stubbs, Paul, and Siniša Zrinščak. 2007. "Croatia." In *Social Policy and International Interventions in South East Europe*, edited by Bob Deacon and Paul Stubbs. Cheltenham: Edward Elgar, 85–102.

Stubbs, Paul, and Siniša Zrinščak. 2011. "Rethinking Clientelism, Governance and Citizenship in Social Welfare: the case of Croatia." Paper presented to ESPANET conference, Valencia. http://espanet2011.files.wordpress.com/2011/08/st3a_stubbs-zrinscak_op.pdf. Accessed March 13, 2012.

Szalai, Julia. 2005. "Poverty and the Traps of Post-communist Welfare Reforms in Hungary: A Fourth World of Welfare Capitalism on the Rise." Paper presented at the Annual Conference of RC19, ISA on "Retheorizing Welfare States: Restructuring States, Restructuring Analysis" Northwestern University, Chicago, September 8–10, 2005.

Szikra, Dorottya. 2004. "The Thorny Path to Implementation: Bismarckian Social Insurance in Hungary in the Late 19th Century." *European Journal of Social Security* 6.3. 255–272.

Tokes, Rudolf. 2000. "'Transitology': global dreams and post-communist realities." *Central European Review* 2(10), http://www.ce-review.org/00/10/tokes10.html. Accessed March 9, 2012.

Tomka, Bela. 2004. *Welfare in East and West: Hungarian Social Security in an International Comparison 1918–1990.* Berlin: Akademie Verlag.

Tridico, Pasquale. 2011. *Institutions, Human Development and Economic Growth in Transition Economies.* Basingstoke: Palgrave Macmillan.

UNDP. 2011. "Beyond Transition: towards inclusive societies." *Regional Human development Report.* UNDP: Bratislava.

UNICEF. 1994. "Crisis in Mortality, Health and Nutrition." *Regional Monitoring Report* 2, UNICEF MONEE Project: Florence.

UNICEF. 1995. "Poverty, Children and Policy: response for a brighter future." *Regional Monitoring Report* 3, UNICEF MONEE Project: Florence.

Venn, Couze. 2006. "A note on assemblage." *Theory, Culture, Society*, Vol. 23, No. 2/3, 107–108.

Verdery, Kathryn. 1996. *What Was Socialism, And What Comes Next?*. Princeton, NJ: Princeton University Press.

Wedel, Janine. 1999. *Collision and Collusion: the strange case of Western aid to Eastern Europe*. Basingstoke: MacMillan.

Wedel, Janine. 2004. "'Studying Through' a Globalizing World: building method through aidnographies." *Ethnographies of Aid: exploring development texts encounters*, edited by Jeremy Gould and Henrik Secher Marcussen. IDS Occasional paper 24, Roskilde University, Denmark.

Williams, Raymond. 1977. *Marxism and Literature*. Oxford: Oxford University Press.

Willis, Paul, and Mats Trondman. 2000. "A Manifesto for Ethnography." *Ethnography* Vol. 1 No. 1, 5–15.

Wolff, Larry. 1994. *Inventing Eastern Europe: The Map of Civilization on the Mind of the Enlightenment*. Stanford University Press.

Yanow, Dora. 2004. "Translating local knowledge at organizational peripheries." *British Journal of Management* Vol. 15, No. 1, 9–25.

Żukowski, Maciej. 2009. "Social Policy Regimes in the European Countries." In *Diversity and Commonality in European Social Policies: The Forging of a European Social Model*, edited by Stanislawa Golinowska, Peter Hengstenberg and Maciej Żukowski. Warsaw: Friedrich-Ebert-Stiftung and Wydawnictwo Naukowe Scholar, 23–32.

Acknowledgements

The extent of my debt to John Clarke, Noémi Lendvai, and David Bainton is, I hope, visible from the text, which borrows substantially from their work and from our diverse collaborations over the years. Notwithstanding our disagreements, including those noted here, Bob Deacon and I continue to enjoy a friendship and a collaboration which enriches everything I write. In Croatia, joint work with Siniša Zrinščak, in particular, forges new understandings of the ways in which transnational and local processes intersect.

Chapter 2
Translations in social policy making

Yun Tae Kim

(3) The Making of the Welfare State in Korea: Policy Discourses and Strategies

Abstract This chapter deals with the competing discourses and strategies that have influenced the development of welfare systems and the expansion of welfare expenditure in South Korea. The author evaluates the institutional consequences of welfare reform in Korea and analyzes the underlying nature of welfare state transformation in relation to Western experiences.

1. Introduction

The welfare state in Korea has developed since the 1960s from limited welfare programs toward more comprehensive welfare systems. This process has resulted in the welfare state in Korea having rather unique characteristics, many of which it has in common only with other East Asian countries. Numerous scholars have argued that an important feature of the evolution of social policy in East Asia has been "welfare developmentalism," which views social policy as an instrument for economic development (Goodman and White 1998; Holliday 2000; Kwon 2007). While history has seen a rapid increase in state-provided social expenditure in East Asian countries, the welfare systems of these countries were, paradoxically, established by conservative governments with anti-welfare ideologies (Aspalter 2002). The Korean case is no exception, with social policy being regarded primarily as a highly effective policy instrument for stimulating economic growth during the country's rapid process of industrialization.

Ever since the financial crisis of 1997–1998, unemployment and poverty have emerged as important social and political issues in Korea. Accordingly, the welfare system has rapidly developed and social spending has dramatically increased since the late 1990s. Owing to the fact that the welfare programs that developed under the Korean "developmental state"[1] turned out to be ineffective, the

1 In general, the term "developmental state" refers to a state that, guided by some kind of plan or strategic goal, sets out to promote national development by means of institutionalized arrangements of policy intervention, and that chooses to play a central role in the process of development (Evans 1995; Weiss and Hobson 1995; Woo-Cumings 1999; Kim 1999).

Korean government had to set up social security systems for the most vulnerable social groups. The Kim Dae Jung (1998–2002) and Roh Moo Hyun (2003–2005) governments both developed more comprehensive welfare systems of social security, public assistance, and social services. As these governments introduced comprehensive welfare systems, part of the responsibility for social welfare began to gradually shift from families and employers to the state.

In this article, I argue that social policy in Korea has developed the unique characteristics of the welfare state, in particular of a "developmental welfare state" (Kwon 2007; Lee and Ku 2007; Dostal 2010), and that it has been transformed into a more comprehensive welfare state since the late 1990s. I examine the competing discourses and strategies that have influenced the development of welfare systems and the expansion of welfare expenditure in Korea. I go on to evaluate the institutional consequences of welfare reform in Korea and analyze the underlying nature of welfare state transformation in relation to Western experiences. Finally, I consider Korea's prospects of achieving its developmental social policy goals and of providing all its citizens with social security.

2. Competing discourses and strategies relating to the welfare state

It is widely acknowledged that state intervention was an indispensable condition for achieving industrial transformation in East Asia. Economic success in Korea was due largely to developmental state policies, which played a strategic role in the country's rapid process of industrialization (Amsden 1989; Wade 1990; White 1988; Woo-Cumings 1999). Apart from economic policy, social policy also played an important role in the national strategy of economic development. Measured against the development of Western European welfare state regimes, East Asian countries, including Korea, introduced social security systems at a time when they found themselves at a relatively low level of economic development (Hort and Kuhnle 2000: 167–168). In 1961, Korea's GDP per capita was about 89 dollars. This shows that Korea and East Asian countries utilized the social welfare systems as policy instruments for economic development. The East Asian welfare states were incorporated into a national strategy for economic development: a developmentalist ideology that subordinated welfare to economic efficiency, discouraged dependence on the state, promoted private sources of welfare, and diverted financial resources from investment in social insurance to investment in infrastructure (Goodman and White 1998: 17). The developmental welfare state in Korea can be regarded as an example of the use of social policy in the process of economic development.

In early 1960s Korea, pursuing the national goals for economic development resulted in a welfare state that operated social insurance schemes for industrial workers in large-scale enterprises. Only a small number of workers had access to this form of social protection which thus failed to extend to many of the most vulnerable groups in the population. While the government enacted social welfare legislation and subsequently worked towards maintaining the social insurance system as such, it failed to invest sufficient resources in the actual provision of social protection. The social insurance systems were managed by governmental agencies, which, though not formally governmental bodies, were strictly controlled by the government.

Since social welfare systems in Korea have focused mainly on industrial workers of large-scale enterprises, the Korean welfare state has, in fact, produced greater social inequality. While high-income earners in the state sector and employees of large-scale enterprises benefited from the social welfare system, vulnerable social groups were exposed to various social risks and had to endure poor living conditions (Kwon 1997). The unemployed were forced to take up work in the self-employed small business sector and the urban informal sector. The poorest members of the population and the disabled are stigmatized by being excluded from the social welfare system. The government has maintained a conservative and selective welfare system and ignored the social rights of the broader population. These characteristics of the welfare state in Korea are well summarized by the notion of the "developmental welfare state," wherein state bureaucrats set economic development as the national goal and utilize social policy as an instrument to accomplish economic targets. While the developmental welfare state pursues social policies and features institutional arrangements that commonly pertain to social welfare systems, it ultimately subordinates them to realizing economic development (Gough 2001).

The developmental utilization of social policy is not a genuinely new phenomenon in connection with the welfare state. The historical example is Bismarck's introduction of social insurance systems in Germany in the 1880s, which was pursuing rapid industrialization through social policy reform while simultaneously aiming to dismantle the socialist labor movement of the time. The fundamental values of human dignity, social justice, and the development of human potential cannot be said to have been indispensable to the Bismarckian welfare system. Rather, the conservative Prussian state was concerned only about its national competitiveness based on industrial and military power, and sought the political compliance of industrial workers to that end. The developmental welfare state in Korea during the period of the country's rapid industrialization can be regarded as a kind of Bismarckian, conservative welfare state.

In the history of the welfare state, there is another well-known take on the developmental use of social policy: the Scandinavian model, in which a universal welfare system operates alongside an active labor market policy. In providing universal welfare benefits and services, this model is designed to provide all citizens with adequate education and skills to enable them to enter the labor market, and consequently to contribute to economic development. The social investment strategy of the Swedish welfare state resulted in dynamic economic development. However, the Scandinavian model has faced serious difficulties with the economic liberalization of the world economy and the ideological shift toward neo-liberalism in economic policies since the 1990s. The important characteristics of this Scandinavian model can be defined as productive welfare, social investment, universal welfare, and social partnership, while the Bismarckian model has all the characteristics of conservative welfare, occupational social insurance, selective welfare, and authoritarian control. It can be said that the welfare state in Korea before the 1997 financial crisis was closer to the Bismarckian conservative model. But recent welfare reforms have yielded a different picture.

Since the 1990s, the ongoing debates on the welfare state and social policy in Europe, responding to the new challenges[2] faced by the traditional neo-Keynesian welfare state settlement, have emphasized the value of "social investment," alongside de-regulation and greater flexibility, as a way of achieving both economic growth and social integration (Taylor-Gooby 2004). Patterns of welfare reform since the late 1990s have been very complex and reflect differing national circumstances. It can be pointed out that there is a discernible general shift toward deregulation, constraints on entitlements to passive benefits, programs to enhance employment, particularly among single parents and young people, targeted subsidies for low earners, and case management. This welfare reform agenda coincided with the rise of "Third Way" politics in European states. The "third way of social democracy" was proposed by Anthony Giddens and New Labor as a policy alternative to meet the novel challenges.

---

2 Current socio-economic transformations that have brought into existence post-industrial labor markets and family structures are generating new social needs and demands, labeled "new social risks" (NSRs). These include facing difficulties in balancing work and family life, having to raise children in single parent families, suffering long-term unemployment, and belonging to a growing number of working poor (Taylor-Gooby 2004). These new social risks tend to be higher among women, the young, and low-skilled workers.

The debates about Third Way politics also made themselves felt in Korean policies regarding the welfare state. When Kim Dae Jung took power in 1998, the government attempted to strike a compromise between traditional statism and market fundamentalism. The Kim Dae Jung government pursued social and economic reforms influenced by the Third Way politics of the Clinton and Blair administrations. The Third Way focused on the fundamental values of equality of opportunity, responsibility, and community, and struck a compromise between economic efficiency and social equality. The details of Third Way policies included introducing lower tax rates for business, pursuing sound fiscal policy, and engaging in welfare reform through the "welfare to work" programs. Such policy proposals have been implemented in Britain, Germany, and the Netherlands, though in different ways. Some left-wing critics have argued, however, that Third Way politics was tantamount to the abandonment of social democratic principles and closer to neo-liberal economic policies.

In general, social policies and labor market policies in Europe have put an emphasis on deregulation and negative activation rather than on social investment and activation (Merkel 2008). Countries boasting high growth and employment rates took different routes to achieving these goals: The Swedish welfare state is a closely integrated social democratic welfare state with high spending on benefits and training programs, while the UK has a more liberal, market-oriented system with lower spending, highly targeted benefits, and less social protection. Differences in welfare development in national contexts are closely related to the historical path dependence that has emerged in various welfare regimes over the last several decades. Although most countries in Europe are keen to implement activation policies for welfare reform, the actual process has varied depending on national social relations, institutional heritage, and political dynamics (Bonoli 2005).

It is true that the Korean government under Kim Dae Jung has learned the lessons of these European experiences. The Kim Dae Jung government has placed emphasis on investment in education, research and development (R&D), and job training and benefit programs in order to enhance job mobility. Education standards have continued to improve, but research and development spending has become more restricted. The government has failed to develop substantial activation programs to support job mobility. Labor market policies have been mostly about resolving conflicts between workers and employers. A steady decline in the influence of the trade unions went hand in hand with a more general, rapid trend toward more flexibility. While the government pursued policies geared toward productivity agreements and greater work flexibility in firms and undertook reforms of passive social security systems, there was no noticeable shift toward supporting more ambitious investment and activation policies. As a consequence, Korea has been beset by considerable social problems.

3. The political dynamics of the welfare state

Following the 1997 financial crisis, the Kim Dae Jung government increasingly supported free-market liberalism. It openly accepted that the only way for Korea to overcome the financial crisis was by promoting competition and foreign investment, introducing a more flexible labor market, and strengthening antitrust laws and their enforcement (Kim, 2005). The government's liberal, free-market reforms faced opposition from the trade unions because greater labor flexibility resulted in large-scale unemployment and social instability. The Kim Dae Jung government sought a class compromise between employers and trade unions which would allow liberal market reforms to be put in place while providing unions with social security systems. As seen in the book *DJnomics* (1998) published by the Kim Dae Jung government, the government openly suggested that the Korean economic system follow the German model of social market economy.[3] This showed that the fundamental logic of the Kim Dae Jung government was to pursue economic and social reform. It increased public social expenditure to help the unemployed and the poor, who suffered most from the effects of the financial crisis.

While Korean social expenditure had risen slowly since the 1960s, it increased sharply after 1998. With the 1997 financial crisis, economic recovery became the national agenda. The US government demanded labor flexibility, which was expected to lead to massive layoffs in most corporations. After President Kim Dae Jung met David Lipton, Under Secretary of the US Treasury, his government promised to accept the liberalization policy package. On the other hand, the Kim Dae Jung government established social safety net programs requiring more government expenditure, in spite of IMF-imposed fiscal restraints. Since the welfare state was mainly composed of compulsory social insurance systems financed by contributions from citizens and employers, government expenditure accounted for less than half of total social expenditure. Since the financial crisis,

---

3 The *ordoliberal* model proposed by the Freiburg School in 1940s Germany put strong emphasis on the government's role in maintaining order in the market economy. *Ordoliberalism* highlights both the need for government intervention to reinforce market economy and the government's active role in the social welfare of every citizen.

however, government expenditure on social welfare, as well as total expenditure on social welfare, has risen sharply. Public social expenditure as a percentage of GDP has increased from 3.7 in 1997 to 7.6% in 2007. The share of welfare expenditure as a percentage of total government spending rose from 17.9% in 1997 to 26.3% in 2007.

The expansion of the Korean welfare system during the late 1990s was comparable to the expansion of American welfare programs during the time of the Great Depression, which ultimately facilitated the establishment of the American welfare system. The Korean experience of welfare expansion refutes the assumption that governments confronted with a financial crisis and exposed to the adverse effects of globalization will refrain from increasing the welfare budget and expanding welfare programs. The Korean case might be said to constitute a "paradox" of welfare expansion in an era marked by financial crises and the adverse effects of globalization (Shin 2000).

The Kim Dae Jung government pursued the two fundamental values of "democracy" and "market economy" by promoting social consensus between employers and trade unions. In January 1998, the Kim Dae Jung government established a tripartite commission, staffed by trade unionists, employers, and government representatives, to tackle labor and social issues. The tripartite commission came to a social agreement to resolve the problems of labor market and welfare reform in the face of the economic crisis. The social agreement spelled out plans to restructure the chaebol, increase labor market flexibility, and implement comprehensive social security measures both for the unemployed and for workers, ultimately resulting in the development of a welfare state. Though some radical trade unions, among them the KCTU (Korean Confederation of Trade Unions), resisted negotiations with business and the government, the Kim Dae Jung government ultimately succeeded in dealing with the demands of workers and organized labor. Its efforts to create social harmony made the government shift toward a more comprehensive social welfare system.

It is also important to note that civil society organizations played an important role in establishing Korean welfare institutions. They formed coalitions advocating more inclusive social policy, and successfully demanded an expansion of social protection to the poor and to other vulnerable groups in society. The passing of the law establishing the National Basic Livelihood Security (NBLS) system in particular goes back to demands from the part of civil society organizations, foremost among them the PSPD (People's Solidarity for Participatory Democracy), to introduce such a public assistance program. It was obvious that the developmental welfare state in its then shape would not be able to cope with the vast number of social challenges confronting it in this time of economic crisis. It was unable to tackle high unemployment, for example, since it presupposed high growth and full employment.

Civil society organizations, such as the PSPD, issued strong demands for more comprehensive social insurance and a more generous welfare system. Employment insurance, offering unemployment benefits and training programs, was expanded in terms of both its coverage and the benefits it provided and a new scheme of social assistance, the NBLS, was introduced to replace the old Livelihood Protection Act (LPA). In addition, the formerly fragmented system of national health insurance was integrated into a National Health Insurance (NHI) Corporation. Through this process, the concept of social rights became an important principle of the welfare state as well as of economic development. Although Korean social expenditure is about 7.5% of GDP, half that of Japan and the US, and one of the lowest among OECD countries, the developmental welfare state in Korea has transformed into a more inclusive developmental welfare state.

The Kim Dae Jung government implemented social policy reforms to effectuate a shift toward a more inclusive developmental welfare state. Such policy changes were strongly influenced by economic considerations. After all, measures of economic liberalization to handle the financial crisis, particularly those geared toward increasing labor flexibility, had lead to a significant increase in the number of unemployed. However, the government's measures to boost social protection ultimately proved too weak to deal with the rise in unemployment: Even though the main social security system for workers had been expanded to no longer apply exclusively to those employed at large-scale corporations, unemployment benefits were simply too low. Public assistance for the poor was equally limited due to a strict means test. In the labor market, the sharp increase in the number of non-regular workers, who came to constitute more than one-third of the overall number of employees, had negative consequences for both economic growth and social equality.

In the face of the financial crisis, income inequality increased sharply, and was to remain high even after the economy recovered from the recession. The Gini ratio fell from 0.31 in 1985 to 0.28 in 1993, remained relatively stable between 1993 and 1997, and then rapidly rose from 0.28 in 1997 to 0.32 by 1999. It fell slightly in the year after that, but still remained at a high 0.3174. This rapidly growing trend of increasing income inequality was closely related to the rise in the unemployment rate. It has been well documented that the unemployment rate soared during the economic recession following the financial crisis. The average unemployment rate in 1998 was 6.8%, 4.2% points higher than in the previous year. Job insecurity had an even more devastating effect on the living conditions of lower-income groups.

The development of the Korean welfare state was to a large extent influenced by social protests relating to political democratization in general and the size of social expenditure in particular, as well as by party competition in democratic elections, the strategic decisions of policy makers (Kim 1999), and the changing role of women. Social and demographic factors, such as an increasingly aging population and an increase in single-parent families, do not cause welfare state expansion in and of themselves. But they do cause street protests, and street protests will convince any government, provided it has ruled out the use of force, to implement social welfare measures. Moreover, many politicians, anxious to win elections, engage with welfare issues for strategic reasons, which they would not do were there no electoral competition between candidates and parties. That being said, governments wanting to promote social welfare would, of course, be well advised to take action before major social protests occur, or before they have lost an election (Aspalter 2002).

In talking about the expansion of the Korean welfare state, it is important to note that the extension of welfare provision was, ultimately, limited in nature. In particular, the extension of social security programs was in the main an attempt to promote industrial competitiveness and economic development. The Kim Dae Jung government openly supported the notion of "productive welfare," and ultimately maintained its characteristic productivist outlook on social policy (Kwon and Holliday 2007: 241). The Roh Moo Hyun government also took up a productivist social policy, proposing a "social investment state" that was influenced by the discourses of Giddens and Blair. From the social democratic perspective, of course, the point of productive welfare is not to institute a welfare state, but to set up a safety net welfare system in line with neo-liberal thought. It can be argued that the Kim Dae Jung government maintained the developmental logic of the welfare state while rapidly expanding welfare expenditure.

4. The institutional consequences of the welfare state in Korea

Do recent welfare developments in Korea point toward a Western-style welfare state? The expansion of the welfare system under the Kim Dae Jung and Roh Moo Hyun governments resulted in a huge growth in social expenditure, taking the average annual growth rate of public social expenditure up to an astonishing 17.51%. However, despite the extension of income security programs and the remarkable rise in social spending, the Korean welfare state had its drawbacks. First, public social expenditure was still very limited in volume. The proportion of public social expenditure to GDP was 5.2% in 1998, right after the 1997 financial crisis. It increased to 6.3% in 1999, and thereafter the ratio of public social expenditure continued to rise. In spite of the introduction of new social security and welfare programs such as the NBLS, government budget allocated to social services was still far below OECD average. The NBLS introduced the concept of "workfare," which is similar to the notion of "welfare to work", in response to concerns over disincentives to work (Kim 2001). The NBLS also includes a clause on family support which stipulates that family members have a legal obligation to support recipients of NBLS benefits. As a combined effect of this rather strict rule and an equally strict means test, only about 3% of the population are actually covered by the NBLS.

Table 1: Annual social welfare expenditure in Korea, 1990–2008

(Unit: a hundred million won, %)

Year	Total		Public Welfare (A)	Mandatory private social expenditure (B)	Voluntary private social expenditure (C)
	Amount	A+B+C			
1990	6,141	3.29	2.91	0.27	0.11
1995	22,524	5.65	3.33	0.32	2.00
2000	45,134	7.48	4.74	0.74	2.00
2005	75,513	8.73	6.42	0.57	1.73
2006	88,981	9.79	7.30	0.58	1.91
2007	98,650	10.12	7.48	0.59	2.05
2008	112,172	10.95	8.30	0.61	2.05
Average	17.51		16.50	14.98	29.43

Source: Koh (2010)

Second, the social safety net for non-standard workers (temporary and part-time workers) is not at all well institutionalized. Income security programs leave a considerable portion of people without any social protection. A rapid increase in non-standard workers has contributed to rising inequality. The growing number of temporary workers has meant an expansion in the number of low-wage workers and of the working poor. IMF demands for increased labor market flexibility gave rise to new types of employment, such as temporary employment and short-term contract employment, and the number of low-wage temporary workers increased by more than 10% between 1997 and 2007. Of those contingent workers, only 42.5% are covered by social insurance programs, as compared to almost three quarters, namely 74.9%, of full-time workers. Such figures are the result of a mismatch between the traditional social insurance system and the new, flexible labor market (Yang 2003). They are highly problematic in that contingent workers not only have to struggle with low wages, but also suffer from limited social protection.

Third, the Korean social security system has limited redistribution effects in that it is mainly concerned with full-time employees at large firms. Korea's Gini coefficient is considerably higher than OECD average, as is its degree of relative poverty. Taxes and contributions to social security systems have little effect on lowering the Gini coefficient. In fact, due to the unequal coverage of full-time and contingent workers, the social welfare system has actually worked toward increasing social and economic inequality by widening the income gap between these two kinds of workers.

The Korean welfare state is facing more pressures and challenges than ever before. The increase in the number of contingent jobs, coupled with the "dualization" of the job market, has had a negative effect on family cohesion by making it more difficult than ever to balance paid work with family responsibilities. This has resulted in the lowest fertility rate Korea has ever seen, and in a quickly aging society. To make things worse, the "old social risks" that many families habitually faced, such as illness, unemployment, and retirement, have far from disappeared, but have instead come to be intertwined with the so-called "new social risks" caused by changes in the labor market, population structure, and family relations. The Korean social welfare system has not, on the whole, been able to manage the new social risks as required. It has failed to reduce economic and overall social inequality. This is perhaps little surprising, given that the social welfare programs introduced by the Kim Dae Jung government in the late 1990s were primarily designed to provide a minimal level of social safety with a view to preventing mass protests and social unrest.

In recent years, there have been many debates in Korean society about the political issues arising from the crisis of the welfare state. Serious ideological and policy conflicts have arisen between conservatives and progressives with regard to free school lunches and the roles and functions of "selective welfare" versus "universal welfare." The Lee Myung Bak government (2008–2013) and conservative politicians have criticized the opposition's calls for free school lunches as "socialist" and "populist." This shows that their concept of social welfare is based on such conservative ideas as those of a "residual" and "selective" welfare system. Progressive parties and civil society organizations, on the other hand, have argued that free lunch is simply a part of free education, which governments should guarantee their citizens as part of their "basic" and "universal" rights. As Esping-Andersen (1990: 2) has claimed, supporters of selective welfare want a liberal welfare state, while providing universal welfare requires a social democratic welfare state.[4]

It can be said that Korea now has a welfare state. Substantial improvements have been made to the social welfare system since the 1997 financial crisis. Korea has moved toward a system of universal public assistance and has introduced medical insurance and universal pension coverage. However, there is no clear notion of a "universal welfare state" in Korea. Welfare state developments up until the 1980s show Korea to have found itself wedged between the conservative-corporatist and liberal models as described by Esping-Anderson. Indeed, it has often been argued that the Korean welfare state was formed as part of economic development policies.

So has the Korean welfare state succeeded in reducing poverty and inequality? It must be said that it has not, as it has not managed to deal adequately with the challenges faced. These include the new social risks related to labor market structure, population structure, and recent shifts in family relations. While the absolute poverty rate has decreased significantly, the rates of relative poverty and inequality have substantially increased since the 1997 financial crisis. The income gap between the lowest and the highest income groups has widened significantly. Overall, there is little doubt that the Korean welfare state lags behind other OECD member countries. There is just as little doubt, however, that the expansion of social insurance and public assistance signified a great step forward for Korea. While the existence of a Korean welfare state is by now beyond questioning, the crucial next step is to decide which model of welfare is more appropriate to meeting the challenges ahead for the Korean welfare state: the "residual" or the "institutional" model. New social risks can no longer be solved by old welfare programs.

5. Future challenges

Over the last few decades, the Korean welfare state has developed at remarkable pace. Economic growth has been relatively stable, exceptional cases such

---

4 The Danish sociologist Esping-Andersen categorizes welfare states into three regime types, or "worlds," of welfare capitalism, namely social democratic, liberal, and conservative-corporatist (Esping-Andersen 1990). In order to define a welfare regime, Esping-Andersen uses two major dimensions, namely the level of decommodification and the type of stratification. Based on the above criteria, he identifies three ideal regime types – liberal, conservative-corporatist, and social-democratic – that will emerge depending on the respective historical and political developments in a given society.

as the 1997 financial crisis aside. Ever since that crisis, public social expenditure has risen dramatically. But Korea has a strong productivist tradition, that is, an approach toward social spending that emphasizes the role of social policy as a tool for economic development. It also has a strong tradition of family support, meaning that family plays an important role in providing private welfare. As a result, Korea is better described as being made up of multiple welfare *societys* than as being a single, universal welfare *state*.

Not unlike European countries, Korea currently faces serious pressures from economic and financial globalization, the transfer of lower-skilled jobs, the emergence of non-traditional family forms, and a rapidly aging population. Demands for better social services to enable working mothers to achieve "work/life balance" and pursue careers are currently less emphatic than in the West, but they are growing stronger. Political debates have been accelerated by public expectations of better social services, which have become sensitive issues. While European countries have moved closer to an East Asian productivist tradition of social spending, there are pressures in East Asia to expand social spending in directions previously developed in Europe.

Recent developments in Korean welfare institutions have raised issues concerning their impact on equality and social justice. A considerable proportion of the workforce remain in unstable, non-standard jobs, and a high proportion of unemployed people and pensioners remain uncovered by national pension systems. It should be noted that social spending is relatively low and directed in ways that have little impact on poverty among older people or people of working age. The problems involved in addressing inequality suggest that social investment strategies need to be set in a context where there are benefits to support the poor of working age, the elderly, and disabled people.

More substantial changes are required in the years ahead to tackle the risk of growing inequality. Among the developments in Europe that might be relevant in this regard, there is a growth of interest in "activation", that is, in measures that encourage a high degree of mobility between jobs, such as offering additional training and attractive benefits (Taylor-Gooby 2004). These approaches are intended to foster a dynamic labor market with a good level of welfare benefits. The second issue concerns government action to ensure equal opportunities for men and women and greater support for mothers in employment. The Korean government needs to follow European examples and pass legislation to establish equal opportunities and parent-friendly workplace practices. It also ought to allocate substantial resources to investing in child care, both by providing public child care and subsidizing private spending on child care. Measures to activate women and create equal opportunities for them already take up substantial resources, but are yet to reach the levels required to reduce, and prevent, poverty through social spending. Government programs aiming to activate women and to create equal opportunities for them invariably require substantial resources if they are to effectively reduce poverty through spending on welfare benefits. For this reason, social investment strategies and activation policies might be particularly appropriate in the Korean context.

References

Amsden, Alice. 1989. *Asia's Next Giant: South Korea and Late Industrialization.* Oxford: Oxford University Press.

Aspalter, Christian. 2002. *Discovering the Welfare State in East Asia.* Westport: Praeger.

Bonoli, Giuliano. 2005. "The politics of the new social policies: Providing coverage against new social risks in mature welfare states." *Policy & Politics,* Vol. 33, No. 3. 431–449.

Briggs, Asa. 1961. "The Welfare State in Historical Perspective." *Archives Europeennes de sociologie,* Vol. 2. 221–258.

Esping-Andersen, Gosta. 1990. *The Three Worlds of Welfare Capitalism.* Princeton: Princeton University Press.

Evans, Peter. 1995. *Embedded Autonomy.* Princeton: Princeton University Press.

Goodman, Roger, and Gordon White. 1998. "Welfare Orientalism and the Search for an East Asian Welfare Model" In *The East Asian Welfare Model: Welfare Orientalism and the State*, edited by R. Goodman, G. White & H. J. Kwon. London: Routledge.

Goodman, Roger, White, Gordon, and Huck-ju Kwon. 1998. *The East Asian Welfare Model: Welfare Orientalism and the State.* London: Routledge.

Gough, Ian. 2001. "Globalization and Regional Welfare Regimes: The East Asian Case." *Global Social Policy* 1.2. 163–189.

Hort, Sven, and Stein Kuhnle. 2000. "The coming of East and South-East Asian welfare states." *Journal of European Social Policy,* Vol. 10, No. 2. 162–184.

Kim Yeon-Myung. 2001. "Welfare state or social safety nets? Development of the social welfare policy of the Kim Dae-Jung administration." *Korea Journal* 41. 169–201.

Kim, Yun Tae. 1999. "Neoliberalism and the Decline of the Developmental State." *Journal of Contemporary Asia,* Vol. 29, No. 2. 441–461.

Kim, Yun Tae. 2005. "*DJnomics* and the Transformation of Developmental State." *Journal of Contemporary Asia,* Vol. 35, No. 4. 471–484.

King, Desmond S. 1999. *In the name of liberalism: illiberal social policy in the USA and Britain.* Oxford: Oxford University Press.

Koh, K., et al. 2010. *Korea's Health and Welfare Trends.* Seoul: KIHASA. (in Korean)

Kwon, Huck-ju. 1997. "Beyond European Welfare Regimes: comparative perspectives on East Asian Welfare systems." *Journal of Social Policy,* Vol. 26, No. 4. 467–484.

Kwon, Huck-ju. 1999. *The Welfare State in Korea: The Politics of Legitimation.* London: Macmillan.

Kwon, Huck-ju. 2007. *Transforming the Developmental Welfare State in East Asia.* London: UNRISD/Palgrave.

Kwon, Soonman, and Ian Holliday. 2007. "The Korean welfare state: A paradox of expansion in an era of globalization and economic crisis?" *International Journal of Social Welfare,* Vol. 16, No. 3. 242–248.

Holliday, Ian. 2000. "Productivist Welfare Capitalism: Social Policy in East Asia." *Political Studies,* Vol. 48, No. 4. 706–723.

Lee, Yih-Jiunn and Yeun-wen Ku. 2007. "East Asian Welfare Regimes: Testing the Hypothesis of the Developmental Welfare State." *Social Policy & Administration,* Vol. 41, No. 2. 197–212.

Merkel, Wolfgang, Petring, Alexander, Henkes, Christian, and Christoph Egle. 2008. *Social Democracy in Power: The Capacity to Reform.* London: Routledge.

Park, Bae-gyoon. 2001. "Labour regulation and economic change: a view on the Korean economic crisis." *Geoforum,* Vol. 32, No. 1. 61–75.

Pierson, Paul. 1995. *Dismantling the welfare state? Reagan, Thatcher, and the politics of retrenchment.* Cambridge: Cambridge University Press.

Shin, Dong-Myeon. 2000. "Financial Crisis and Social Security: the Paradox of the Republic of Korea". *International Social Security Review,* Vol. 53. 83–107.

Taylor-Gooby, Peter. 2004. "New risks and social change." In *New risks, new welfare: The transformation of the European welfare state,* edited by Peter Taylor-Gooby. Oxford: Oxford University Press, 1–28.

Wade, Robert. 1990. *Governing the market: economic theory and the role of government in East Asian industrialization.* Princeton: Princeton University Press.

Weiss, Linda, and Hobson, John M. 1995. *States and Economic Development: A Comparative Historical Analysis*. Cambridge: Polity.

White, Gordon (ed.). 1988. *Developmental States in East Asia*. New York: St Martin's.

Woo-Cumings, Meredith (ed.). 1999. *The Developmental State*. Ithaca: Cornell University Press.

Yang, Jae-jin. 2000. "The Rise of the Korean Welfare State amid Economic Crisis, 1997–99: Implications for the Globalisation Debate." *Development Policy Review*, Vol. 18. 235–256.

Myung Joon Park

(4) Micro-Policy Translation and Policy Entrepreneurship in the Transformation of Korean Welfare Capitalism

Abstract Applying the analytical concept of *translation* the author presents a case study on the Emergence of the Employment Insurance System (EIS), a social insurance program established in the wake of democratization designed to guarantee the livelihoods of workers in times of unemployment as an example for decision-making processes in South Korean welfare policy.

1. Introduction

As a young democracy and emerging welfare state in East Asia, South Korea has experienced profound changes in its labor market institutions over recent decades, starting in the late 1980s in the wake of democratization. Some institutional arrangements were newly adopted, while existing ones were significantly strengthened.[1] A large number of studies have dealt with these dynamics.[2] Many of them have interpreted the emergence or replacement of certain welfare programs as the outcome of rational calculation by a government aiming to utilize such programs for political purposes.[3] The logical connection between institutional changes and their political- or macro-economic context enables us to understand why certain changes occurred at a certain point in time. However, such a macro-factor-based explanation places limits on our understanding of

1 Prior to these arrangements, the authoritarian state in Korea had established other institutional mechanisms for social welfare, such as the national health care system, the industrial accident protection system, the public assistance program in the 1960s, and the national pension program in the 1970s. Although all of these institutions were designed to function only for specific groups of the Korean population, and even though their implications were largely trivial, the basic concepts and institutional structures of the emerging Korean welfare state were all formed before democratization and were merely reformed and strengthened as of the late 1980s.

2 See, for example, Kwon (1999), Shin (2003), and Hwang (2006).

3 Indeed, when major social welfare programs are launched by authoritarian states, this is usually done with a view to influencing election results or bringing about specific political changes.

why specific changes occurred; in other words, it cannot explain why specific institutional elements were revised or replaced, or why specific elements were freshly adopted as part of new institutions. This study will explore different logics in order to gain a more elaborate understanding of the institutional changes in Korean welfare capitalism, paying special attention to the international flow of knowledge in establishing the new institutions, and to micro-level interactions in the process of institutional reconstruction.

With this purpose in mind, this study will carry out an empirical analysis of the emergence of the Employment Insurance System (EIS), a social insurance program designed to guarantee the livelihoods of workers against unemployment that was established in the wake of democratization. As the first comprehensive mechanism to protect workers against unemployment, its establishment had epoch-making implications for the institutional changes in Korean welfare capitalism. Analyzing the emergence process of the EIS from the perspective of policy translation, this study pays attention to the role of policy experts, those who learned from the experiences and trends of other advanced countries and created their own concept for reform on that basis. These experts were not confined to the role of passive providers and interpreters of knowledge. Rather, some of them were actively engaged in the decision-making process, arguing for their rationales and ideas to be accepted and negotiating with those who were against the EIS – all of which can be understood as an act of policy translation. On account of these experts' creative and active commitment, as well as their invisible, yet effective, contributions, the launch of the EIS could finally be realized, albeit not in the form of a rigorous realization of those experts' original plans. The activities of these experts can be understood as a kind of policy entrepreneurship. Or, in other words, their role as policy translators in establishing the EIS contained elements of policy entrepreneurship.

In this way, the story of the establishment of the EIS offers particularly promising material for a discussion of the mechanisms of policy translation and their implications for institutional change. In sum, this study has three core purposes. First, it tries to prove that the entrepreneurship of policy experts was critical in creating the EIS and formed part of its comprehensive activities of policy translation. Second, it explores the utility of the translation metaphor for analyzing the particular form of welfare capitalism that developed in the still relatively new East Asian democracy that is South Korea. Third, it draws implications from the Korean experience of introducing welfare capitalism in order to discuss what policy translations are and how they can be made to succeed in processes of institutional change.

This study is based on intensive interviews I have conducted with three experts in the field of Korean labor markets in September 2010[4]. In what follows, I will first discuss the techniques of policy translation and then formulate a number of hypotheses for the purposes of empirical analysis, including that of there being a need to distinguish between macro and micro aspects of policy translation. The third section of this contribution analyzes discursive contests regarding the creation of the EIS that can be understood as acts of macro-level policy interpretation. The fourth section analyses policy entrepreneurship, which was crucial to creating the EIS and can be considered as micro-level policy translation. The final part discusses the findings and implications of the analysis.

2. Structures of policy translation and types of policy translators

In a globalized world, whenever new institutions are adopted in a country and old ones are reshaped or replaced, a working knowledge of the policies and institutions of other countries comes to have increasingly significant implications. Faced with the necessities of policy change and institutional reform, policy actors attempting to create alternative programs often look to other countries for inspiration and try to learn about, and analyze, the features, performances, and problems of their programs and systems. In this process of cross-border learning, or of knowledge flowing across borders, stories about the realities operative in other countries are not only copied and delivered, but also reconstructed and re-interpreted. Such a process, which is likely to be active and creative, can be named "policy translation."[5]

Recently, social scientists have paid particular attention to elaborating the policy translation perspective, indicating the limits of previous approaches to the

---

4 One of these interviewees, whom I will refer to us "R.", had been particularly influential in his role as a policy entrepreneur. The other two interviewees, both of whom are research fellows at the Korea Labor Institute (KLI), concurred that R. had been the central figure in designing the EIS. During the interview with the author, R. himself mentioned that he had often been introduced as "the father of the EIS" in developing countries that wanted to learn from the Korean EIS system.

5 The author is of the opinion that policy translations can be extraordinarily dynamic in new democracies or less developed countries when they are attempted with the intention of effecting profound institutional reform. After all, policy translators who are importing policy ideas and institutional elements from advanced democracies are likely to be extraordinarily eager to learn from those advanced democracies.

phenomenon of cross-border knowledge flows, such as “knowledge diffusion” or “policy transfer”. Comparing it with previous approaches, they have emphasized several strengths of the translation perspective (Freeman 2009).

Despite its strengths and validities, the policy translation perspective is still in need of further elaboration, especially as the definition of “policy translation” remains ambiguous. This study is designed to make a contribution to elaborating both the concept and the perspective. Bearing this in mind, I will attempt to discern the concept’s limits and suggest some new “logical settings”, raising two questions in particular concerning the place and the activities of policy translation: Where do policy translations take place? And what exactly is it that policy translators do?

The policy translation perspective assumes that policies are translated in spaces or arenas (two-dimensional), rather than being transferred or diffused through channels (one-dimensional). Policy translations can take place in various places, wherever discursive contests as to the directions and extent of reforms are being conducted. It is a place where advocates and opponents compete with each other, translate the experiences of other countries, draw implications from them, judge the results, and present opinions on the applicability or validity of the reforms for their own countries.

This notion can be further developed. I will make the assumption that policies are translated within a space (three-dimensional) that is structured into multiple levels. Specifically, two levels of policy translation can be distinguished. The first one pertains to macro-level policy translations, which can be conducted in a broad space, such as the public sphere, where competing camps and groups (or macro advocacy coalitions) with differing policy preferences come together to engage in a debate about reform. The second pertains to micro-level policy translation, which occurs in a more concrete space, one in which individuals (crucial bringers of ideas or program makers) compete with one another.

More importantly still than the levels of policy translation, the concrete actions of policy translators need to be examined in further depth. As implied above, policy translators involved in the process of policy translation come from a variety of backgrounds, and they act at different levels. Actors at the macro level are collective actors in the form of certain camps, communities, or coalitions engaged in a set of macro-discursive contests, whereas actors at the micro-level are individuals. In particular, it is also possible to further differentiate actors at the micro level of policy translation. Some of them can play a critical role as *policy entrepreneurs* by actively translating policies in the process of formulating reform concepts. Here, the concept of policy entrepreneurship can be connected with the perspective of policy translation.

In the next two sections, I shall analyze policy translations that occurred in the creation of the EIS in Korea, both at the macro and micro level. In particular, I will examine how the key policy translator mentioned in the introductory section engaged in policy translation at a micro level by way of policy entrepreneurship.

3. Macro-level policy translations and discursive contests

Korean policy actors from the 1960s to the 1980s had a largely negative attitude towards unemployment insurance programs for mostly ideological reasons. To them, unemployment insurance was a product of socialist thought, and therefore was to be rejected. However, from the late 1980s and early 1990s onwards, policy actors became more differentiated in their views and opinions. Some of them started to translate the systems and experiences of other countries in a positive way, and argued for the adoption of certain elements of these experiences in the Korean context. Regardless of this, previous, established notions remained dominant in the public sphere and among the communities of policy experts.

3.1 The dominant ideology on unemployment benefits and negative policy translation

With the beginning of Korean industrialization in the early 1960s, a massive working class was formed, and modern labor markets emerged. It thus became necessary to create institutional mechanisms to protect the livelihoods of workers in periods of unemployment. As part of the package of modern labor laws created immediately after the end of the Korean War in 1953, the Work Standard Act (WSA) contained core instruments to regulate various aspects of labor markets such as working conditions and the recruitment and dismissal of workers. Nevertheless, only very few mechanisms were created to protect workers' livelihoods during periods of unemployment. It was only with the establishment of the EIS in the 1990s that a large pool of funds started to be gathered so that workers' livelihoods could be protected during periods in which they had to seek new employment possibilities – provided that their unemployment was not the result of their own actions.

So, what had hindered the creation of a program like the EIS until the early 1990s? According to the dominant ideology of the Korean developmental state model, it was taboo to adopt policies that would help to provide those who do not work with a means of living. To pay people who do not work an allowance was regarded as a socialist or communist policy. In this framework of interpretation, unemployment benefits were thus translated in a negative way. Moreover, these negative translations were unilaterally produced within the communities of policy makers and in the public sphere. It was considered that such programs would ruin the national economy by reducing the workers' motivation. There was an almost total absence of symmetrical discursive contests affirming the necessity and potential usefulness of labor market regulation. This situation continued for almost three decades, right throughout the era of authoritarian regimes.[6]

3.2 The emergence of discursive contests and competition in policy translations

The establishment of the EIS in the 1990s presupposed an ideological change and a redefinition of the situation of workers in the labor market. The launch of the EIS signaled a dramatic win against its opponents, who found it unnecessary, hazardous, and burdensome. Its creation was accompanied by hard-fought debates between two advocacy coalitions. Their arguments were based on different socio-scientific theories on the mechanisms of labor market institutions and worker behavior. They interpreted differently the experiences and systems of labor market institutions in advanced countries, and the implications of introducing mechanisms to protect workers from unemployment.

The opponents' coalition comprised economic bureaucrats and business leaders. Being against the adoption of programs like the EIS, they were the proponents of the above-mentioned conventional opinion that had prevailed in Korean society throughout the era of rapid industrialization. The EIS' opponents were mostly anxious about the negative effects of such a program on the national economy, maintaining the conventional opinion that only high growth could solve the problem of unemployment. Unemployment benefits were directly identified with economic extravagance or social cost, which would soon erode the national economy and demotivate workers. Holding steadfast to this conventional notion, they underestimated the potential of welfare states in general, and interpreted the effects of unemployment insurance programs negatively and skeptically.

With time, policy experts came to adopt a more differentiated stance. Some began to recognize the functional necessity of programs protecting workers from unemployment. Creating counter-ideas, EIS advocates tried to develop positive translations of Western European experiences.

---

6 The military government carried out an experimental examination in the early 1960s. It explored the possibility and necessity of programs to rescue and support the unemployed. A secret report was made with the title "Examination of the Adoption of Unemployment Insurance." However, it was only a report to the Labor Office Director. No further concrete programs were created (Interview with R.).

There were two kinds of expert groups. One group was ideologically sympathetic with social democracy and workers' social rights, and found it useful to create protective measures for the unemployed. Advocating general improvements to the welfare and social rights of workers by strengthening the relevant institutions, these reform-oriented political leaders – who were mainly positioned in the opposition camp at the time – were leaders of the labor movement and of civil society.

The other group focused on the labor market and, more fundamentally, on the situation of labor in Korea, as well as on capitalism in general. Against the background that economic growth was deteriorating, they shared the idea that the growth-centered model based on developmentalist conservatism would have to be reformed. One central aspect of such reform would be to learn from experiences in advanced industrial countries, and to introduce unemployment insurance in order to be able to cope with the high number of unemployment in a way that would help to stabilize the economy.

In this way, these two advocacy coalitions started to compete with each other, promoting different kinds of employment insurance programs. However, it seemed at the time as if a third group, consisting of an overwhelming number of reactionaries opposing the EIS, would prevail in the struggle over unemployment policies in the late 1980s and early 1990s, just prior to the creation of the EIS. They seemed especially likely to succeed as they disposed of far greater resources in the policy formation process than their opponents did. The EIS was nonetheless enacted. How did this happen? In searching for an answer, I will take a concrete look at the relevant policy-making process.

4. Micro-level policy translation and policy entrepreneurship

The above-described conditions formed the setting in which competing macro-policy translations relating to unemployment policy were produced. They were also the backdrop against which policy entrepreneurs and their micro-policy translations came to play a critical role. This section will attempt to provide a more elaborate analysis of the decisions taken by policy entrepreneur R. R. possessed the particular characteristics of both power and knowledge, and he had previous experience regarding policy translation in the context of unemployment benefits. He chose to actively mobilize his resources in order to advocate and initiate the establishment of the EIS. R. designed the concrete details of the EIS by translating the experiences of advanced countries in light of his subjective evaluation of them. He also actively tried to persuade opponents of the EIS to give up their opposition to the EIS and throw their weight behind supporting it. That being said, R. was ultimately unable to fully realize all of his ideas on account of limited resources.

4.1 The resources of policy entrepreneur R.

Before analyzing R.'s policy translation, it is necessary to list the resources he had at his disposal, and to elucidate their crucial dimensions–resources such as knowledge and intelligence, status and power, an extended personal network, the capacity to inspire trust, and the like.

R. is basically a labor economist. He majored in economics at one of the top three universities in Korea, and passed the national examination to become a higher public servant (*haengcheonggoshi*). In the 1970s and 1980s, he worked at the Economic Planning Board (EPB), which was the core platform for economic policy making, the headquarters that guided Korea through its economic miracle. In the 1980s, R. went to the US to continue his studies, gaining a PhD in labor economics. This significantly enhanced both his knowledge capital and learning capacity. Notably, studying in the US confirmed R. in his initial intuition that Korea would soon need institutions to protect unemployed workers.

Upon his return to Korea, R. was employed as a senior researcher at the Korea Labor Institute (KLI), which was established in 1988 as a government think tank for labor-related affairs and labor policies.[7] The KLI was one of a number of "National Policy Institutes" in Korea (*kukchaekyonkuso*). Throughout the 1990s, researchers employed at these national institutions played a crucial role in shaping and reshaping various other institutions and policies. Some of them were significant actors not only for policy conceptualization in theory or research, but also in the production of actual political discourses and practical knowledge. The role of R. is highly representative of such activities. Moreover, R. was a particularly central and successful figure in this process. Working at the KLI, he played a crucial role in designing and consolidating the EIS, by analyzing Korean labor markets, searching for a way to construct the EIS, carrying out intensive research on functionally equivalent systems in other countries, and, finally, examining what mechanisms should be adopted for Korea.

4.2 R.'s previous experience in policy translation

Although the core period of R.'s activities as a policy entrepreneur and policy translator as regards the EIS coincides with his employment at the KLI, he had

7 When the author interviewed R. in September 2010, R. was a university professor.

already acquired significant experience in related activities while working at the EPB in early 1981. It was then that the Labor Office (*nodongcheong*) was upgraded to the status of Ministry of Labor (MOL) and that the fifth five-year plan of economic development was under revision. At the time, the MOL officially requested the EPB to examine the possibilities of introducing a social insurance program to tackle unemployment. As a young officer at the EPB, R. was put in charge of this work. However, since no reference material on unemployment insurance was to be found at either the MOL or the EPB, and since, more generally speaking, knowledge of the relevant policy considerations was extremely limited in the Korean administration of the time, the examination was, ultimately, never seriously pursued. Furthermore, negative opinions on social insurance systems prevailed among government actors, and did so by a large margin.

> A prejudice prevailed in the Ministries that workers would not work if they could receive money for their livelihoods even though they were not employed. At that time, the Blue House staff took a round trip to Europe and some leading figures argued that unemployment insurance would be hazardous. (Interview with R.)

Under these circumstances, R. was unable to come to a scientifically informed position as to whether, and if so, when, specific labor market programs like the EIS should be introduced.

He agreed with the dominant ideas and opted against a change in policy, finding that it was too early for Korea to adopt such a program in light of the level of its economic development. However, R. did give some serious thought to the idea of unemployment policies and came to the conclusion that it was necessary to forge *some* sort of mechanism to protect unemployed workers and promote employment – even though he stopped short of suggesting the creation of an unemployment benefits program. Based on his general findings, R. suggested that a program be adopted under the name of "employment insurance" (instead of unemployment insurance) which would not provide workers with unemployment benefits, but instead would operate within the frame of employment policies. The name for the program arose spontaneously, since it made inherent sense from the point of view of a labor economist. In terms of content, the program was not based on any systematic study of the experiences and systems of other countries. R. presented his idea to high-ranking members of the EPB, and it was passed on to the Vice Prime Minister in the early 1980s.

Although they were not based on up-to-date knowledge of other countries' labor market policies, but instead on a combination of theoretical expertise and practical necessities, R.'s policy choices at this early stage in the process already included an element of policy translation (passive counter-translation). This early experience provided R. with the decisive momentum to later continue the search for a new and creative way to conceptualize a program to protect workers. This was his first, preliminary policy translation regarding issues later to be addressed by the EIS, and this specific experience was to prove crucial to his subsequent work in designing the latter. It was R.'s first encounter with what would later be the agenda of the EIS and had significant personal implications for him. This was the start of his career as a policy entrepreneur and policy translator in matters related to the EIS.

4.3 Policy entrepreneurship: Self-initiative and resource mobilization

The argument against unemployment benefits prevailed in Korea well into the 1990s. As many European countries were making efforts to reduce the cost of their social welfare programs in the era of globalization, opponents to the EIS thought the time was simply not right for introducing this kind of unemployment insurance system. They witnessed the reduction and malfunctioning of welfare states in Europe, coupled with the rise of neo-conservatism that had already started in the 1980s, and were aware of the fact that welfare states in advanced economies were beginning to put more emphasis on productivity and competitiveness. Under the influence of this knowledge, key actors were skeptical about the creation of the EIS in the early 1990s. As a result, the launch of the EIS was postponed until the final phase of the 7th five-year plan of economic development as executed by the following government. One of the main reasons for the postponement can be seen in the objections of business leaders and economic bureaucrats (*Dongailbo 22 Feb 1991, p. 22*). Even after the EPB and the MOL had finally made a decision to implement the EIS, the Ministry of Commerce, Industry and Energy (MOCIE) expressed fundamental objections to its introduction, along with the leaders of Korea's major businesses (*Segyeilbo 29 August 1991, p. 9*).

In this situation, R. endeavored for several months to persuade the powerful opponents of the EIS to change their minds, being convinced of the importance of introducing it. At this time, the task of examining the adoption of the EIS lay not with the KLI, but with the Korea Health and Society Institute (KOHSI), a government think tank specializing in social policies and welfare programs. However, R. soon found out that the KOHSI was scarcely interested in implementing the policy. According to him, the fact that a body as powerful as the EPB had allocated this task to the KOHSI was highly indicative of its reluctance to undertake the task itself. R. strongly argued for EIS-related work to be done by the KLI itself, which ultimately led the KOHSI to hand responsibility for examining the adoption of the EIS back to the government. It was transferred to the KLI in March 1991.

From then on, a discussion on the adoption of the EIS began in earnest, and R. came to be directly involved with planning related to the EIS. R. established a special body at the KLI, namely the Employment Insurance Planning Unit (EIPU), or *koyongpoheomkihoiktan*, designed to deal efficiently with matters related to the EIS, a body in which he played the most important role. He organized and led discussions attended by labor organizations, business organizations, other technocrats, and experts. He acted as a genuine entrepreneur, and even went so far as to invest his own private financial resources into the project, as the EIPU was not receiving enough financial support at the time. Moreover, he personally conducted contract research work and spent the money he thus earned on managing the EIPU.

> We never received even a single Won from the government. The government had previously promised to support us with 300 Million Won, as decided at the Conference of Economy-Related Ministries (CERM). But the MOL never received the hundreds of millions of Won. I was the one who earned the money and invested it into the management of the EIPU. (Interview with R.)

4.4 Policy translation: Evaluating and mixing

In terms of functional characteristics, the EIS is unique. It contains tools pertaining to active labor market policies designed to prevent dismissals of workers by supporting employers and promoting workers' skills through vocational training. Thus, two different programs were merged into one: the first was an unemployment benefits program as part of a social insurance system; the other a program geared towards increasing and maintaining active participation in the labor market by promoting vocational training for the jobless and supporting employers who were willing to refrain from dismissing their workers. The combined characteristics of the EIS imply that it was the outcome of several political compromises.

R.'s policy translations in the process of setting up the EIS mainly fall into his time as head of the Employment Insurance Planning Unit (EIPU) at the KLI. In the course of his work there, R. traveled to a number of advanced countries to collect information, and gain knowledge, on systems and policies similar to what he envisaged for Korea in terms of labor market policies and unemployment insurance schemes. His aim in visiting Japan, Sweden, Germany, France, the USA, and Canada, among others, was not to use a specific country as a benchmark, but instead to examine the strong points of each and every country, compare all of them with one another, and draw lessons for Korea from these combined findings.[8] R. also invited experts from four major countries – Japan, the USA, Germany, and the UK – to attend a workshop in Korea. These efforts were all part of his policy translation activities.

In the process of selecting cases and drawing lessons, the personal preferences of the policy entrepreneur will inevitably make themselves felt. That being so, the following questions need to be asked here: What were R.'s original preferences, his positions and opinions? To what extent did he revise them as a consequence of his research trips? And which of the elements he was confronted with did he ultimately choose to incorporate into the EIS? The policy translation process became a process of hybridizing old and new knowledge. According to R., the EIS is not a direct copy of any one country's system of regulating its labor market and catering for the unemployed. Rather, it is a mix mainly of the German, Swedish, and Japanese systems, where so-called active labor market policies had developed in addition to the protective mechanisms of unemployment benefits. R. was personally convinced that the new institution would strengthen elements of the "governance" principle, as democratic administrative mechanisms had first developed in Northern or Continental Europe. In line with this assessment, he deemed the Japanese system inappropriate, since it was based on a "strong state" tradition and thus less democratic in nature. R. found Germany and Sweden to represent ideal cases, while the systems of France and the USA, were, in his view, overly oriented towards unemployment benefits, which is why he sought to avoid following them as best as he could.

4.5 Translation as persuasion: Coping with opponents

As part of his translation activities, R. also had to address counter-arguments brought forward by opponents of the EIS. Since he originally came from a community of economic technocrats, it was relatively easy for him to communicate with and persuade them. As a former member of the opponents' group, he was very well acquainted with the people in that group, as well as their manner of thinking, and had extraordinary personal networks in their community. As he avows: "I had earned the personal trust of those working in the EPB. One of my colleagues there even became a Minister later. The fact that I spoke to them frankly and with sincerity also helped in persuading them to adopt the type of institution I had described."

A certain Deputy Minister of the EPB in the early 1990s, to give an example, was continuously inclined to think, in a prejudiced way, that the EIS would only

8 Through intensive studying, R. became aware of the fact that Japan uses the expression "employment insurance."

result in an increase in unemployment. The MOL thus failed in trying to persuade the economic bureaucrats to establish the program. One day, however, a senior official of the Ministry called R. and expressed his anxiety about the possible consequences of failing to create the EIS. In that situation, R. came to play a critical role and ultimately saved the plans for the introduction of the EIS from failure. For, having listened to the senior MOL official's concerns, R. went to visit the Deputy Minister of the EPB and respectfully asked him to lay out his understanding of the characteristics of the EIS. The Deputy Minister then elaborated on his negative view of the EIS, saying that he thought the program would, in fact, cause the number of unemployed to multiply.

R. took the opportunity to explain the background to the EIS and advocate its essential usefulness, emphasizing that the program was a welcome chance to finally adopt labor market policies in Korea, and that unemployment benefits would not constitute the focal point of this reform. He argued:

> The diseases of the advanced countries were caused by unemployment benefits. We are neither able nor willing to recreate them. Those who find themselves dismissed from the labor markets should receive help in finding further work. Previously, it was thought that economic growth could be able to solve all problems related to employment, but those days are gone. Look at the advanced countries. Their key policies have been unable to reduce unemployment to below 10%. Even though the problems of unemployment will not altogether disappear, we may still be able to *manage* them effectively if we design our institutions well. (Interview with R.)

Thanks to R.'s endeavors, both the Deputy Minister of the EPB and the EPB as a whole came to change their opinions, thereby accelerating the adoption of the EIS.

4.6 The limits of policy translation

It must be noted that, while his actions in first gathering and then supplying information with a view to introducing the EIS had been crucial, R. was, ultimately, unable to realize his plans in exactly the way he wanted to due to his limited influence in the legislative process. When the EIS Act was passed in December 1993, R. criticized it not only for having been passed without any intensive discussions at the National Assembly, but also because it was providing the government with too much power. He tried to persuade the bureaucrats in charge at the Ministry to change the Act, yet no amendments were made. R. found the actors in the government to be chiefly interested in holding on to money.

He thought that the most serious problem of the EIS Act was its similarity with the Japanese system of regulating its labor market and catering for the unemployed. The technocrats in the Ministry of Labor had wanted to follow the latter even though R. had strongly advised against doing so, advocating that the EIS clearly distance itself from the Japanese model. In providing crucial information on the systems of the USA, the UK, and Germany to the technocrats in the MOL, he had also recommended that the Japanese system not be followed. However, it was technically difficult for the Korean technocrats to apply the elements of the US and UK systems to the Korean context, since the US and UK legal systems are totally different to that of Korea, which is, in fact, far more similar to that of Japan. It was thus relatively easy for the technocrats to copy, or closely follow, the Japanese model.[9] As a result, the state-centered path of East Asian economic governance was reproduced in the EIS Act.

5. Discussion

This analysis has examined the role of a policy entrepreneur and his policy translations in the emergence of the EIS. The latter would simply not have come into being without R.'s special efforts, particularly his acts of policy translation. Amongst other things, R. creatively changed the name of the program to EIS, actively organized a unit for research and discussion related to its inception, persuaded opponents of the EIS to give up their opposition and throw their weight behind supporting the EIS by utilizing his extensive networks, and, finally, produced a detailed suggestion for the EIS's design based on a careful analysis of information he had gathered on the systems of other advanced countries. His policy translation therefore made a critical contribution not only to creating the EIS, but also to shaping its characteristics.

This case study of one particular policy entrepreneur, or, to put it otherwise, "policy translator," provides valuable clues to understanding the institutional dynamics of Korean welfare capitalism more generally. Throughout the entire process of institutional reform of Korean welfare capitalism, policy entrepreneurs have put their knowledge and understanding at the service of the public, by informing the legislative process, and, prior to that, initiating, and engaging in, policy-making processes in the role of strategic designers. In the case of Korea, policy entrepreneurs have extraordinarily broad leeway for action, since Korean society is a transitional society in which the capacities of political parties are not yet very pronounced. The task that remains is to develop a systematic understanding of the diverse roles played by policy entrepreneurs and of their effects on the overall process of institutional reform of Korean welfare capitalism.

9 For instance, the MOL simply adopted the Japanese definition of "unemployment".

Meanwhile, this analysis has further implications for the concept of policy translation. By way of conclusion, I shall underscore several significant points about what policy translation is and how it is conducted. These are as follows:

First, institutional changes do not only require a change of power holders, but also a renewal of ideas, that is, the adoption of new policies and the carrying out of novel policy translations. Whenever a paradigmatic change is pursued, whether or not such change will have palpable impact depends on whether or not policy entrepreneurs succeed in *translating* the underpinning policies of such change into institutional reform. This process of translation is especially important in new democracies, in which democratic institutional arrangements are not yet fully established but rather are in the process of being imported from advanced democracies. In such new democracies, contrasting discourses are likely to revolve both around the future direction and the depth of further democratization, while the potential side-effects of novel programs and institutions are also of particular concern.

Second, policy translations are vertically structured and can take place at different levels. For one thing, collective actors who agree on the need for certain policy reforms can decide to participate in discursive contests taking place within the broader public sphere. For another, policy translations can also take place at a lower level, in a smaller space, as in the case of individual actors choosing to compete against each other. In such a setting, acts of policy translation at the lower level will be influenced by acts of policy translation at the higher level.

Third, policy translations are also conducted horizontally within individual discursive contests. As part of the multifaceted process of policy formulation, actors perform acts of policy translation, and in doing so bring to bear their specific ideas, interests, preferences, and judgments. First and foremost, advocates and opponents engaged in discursive contests will each undertake their own policy translations. However, in an arena of discursive contest policy translators will often have to confront, and deal with, the policy translations of their opponents, in other words, the policy translations of those who interpret policy ideas and knowledge in a manner different to theirs. A policy translation heading in one direction will invariably come up against other policy translations heading in other directions. New policies will often be the result of compromise between policy translations originally headed in different directions. Choosing a particular policy idea as a result of discursive contest is akin to choosing a particular set of policy translations.

Fourth, policy translators are active. The process of policy translations is not just a relatively passive process of interpretation, but an active process requiring initiative and the taking of action. Policy translators do more than simply copy and paste; they are actively and creatively involved in reinterpreting policy knowledge. The strategies and resources policy translators choose to draw on will be of central importance to reconstructing policy knowledge and determining the ultimate characteristics of the resulting new policies or institutions. Policy translators will not merely draw on their knowledge, but instead will make equal and active, but more or less visible, use of whatever other resources they might have, such as personal and professional networks, or their status and symbolic capital. In some situations, policy translators can also become policy entrepreneurs.

Fifth, policy translation is a game in an arena of competition for power. A successful policy translator needs to be able not only to read up on, supply, and reinterpret the information relevant to their translation, but also to persuade their opponents, i.e., those who translate that same information into a different policy. Regardless of the objective validity of a particular translation, whether or not one's initiative comes to fruition will depend upon the scale of one's resources in the networks of power and on the degree to which they can be effectively mobilized. Without any substantive power, a policy entrepreneur will not be able to achieve their goal. It may be more difficult for a policy entrepreneur to realize their aims if their policy translation is oriented toward changing a deep-rooted path of current institutional arrangements. In such a case, the policy entrepreneur may well come into sharp conflict with those who are interested in pursuing the given path, and will have to invest heavily in trying to persuade them, or in trying to find other ways of realizing the alternative policy.

References

Kwon, Huck-ju. 1999. *The Welfare State in Korea: The Politics of Legitimation.* London: Palgrave.

Shin, Dong-Myeon. 2003. *Social and Economic Policies in Korea: Ideas, Networks and Linkages.* London: Routledge.

Hwang, Gyu-Jin. 2006. *Pathways to State Welfare in Korea: Interests, Ideas and Institutions* Aldershot: Ashgate.

KLI. 2006. *Employment Insurance in Korea: The First Ten Years*, KLI.

Freeman, Richard. 2009. "What is 'translation'?" *Evidence & Policy: A Journal of Research, Debate and Practice*, Vol. 5, No. 4. 429–447.

Chapter 3
The Translation of legal norms and ideas

Seog-Yun Song

(5) The Transplantation of the German Constitutional Provision on Political Parties in South Korea*

Abstract This chapter analyzes the adoption of the Korean constitutional provision on political parties in the year 1962 as a way of exemplifying the kind of role that the *transplantation* of Western constitutional provisions played in the modernization of developing countries.

1. Introduction

The German theory of the party state (*Parteienstaat*) has substantially influenced post-1960s Korean constitutions, in the process being extended and strengthened to such a degree that the Korean constitution of 1962 even granted political parties a monopoly on all political activity. This tendency to overemphasize the party state, although mitigated nowadays, is still well alive in certain areas of Korean law, such as those pertaining to political parties, elections, and political funding.

A critical analysis will hereinafter be conducted of how the German constitutional provision on political parties (Article 21 of the Basic Law) was transplanted[1] into the Korean constitution. A mere textual comparison of Article 21

---

* This article is a partly abbreviated and supplemented version of Song 2000a: 115–146.

1 There are two reasons why the word "legal transplantation" is used in this article. First, the meaning "to plant elsewhere," which is implicit in the word "transplantation," is value-neutral, and so the word is able to embrace both the term "reception," which can connote the consent and activeness of the receiver, and the term "imposition," in the sense of diffusion of a legal system through coercion. It can therefore ensure the objectivity of the analysis. The term "transplantation" also seems able to stimulate our social scientific imagination, in that it is suggestive not only of the object of transplantation itself (plants, bodily organs, etc.), but also of the correlation of the climate of the place where it originally formed with the one where it is to be newly transplanted. On a recent development of the methodological discussion in the field of comparative law, *see* Perju 2012.
Following discussions during the conference, I came to the conclusion that the term "translation" is not appropriate at least for the purposes of comparative law. The

and the 1962 Constitution would, however, not suffice to achieve the goal of this study. In order to go beyond such a mere textual comparison, and in order to avoid being led into making hasty conclusions, it will first of all be necessary to reconsider the methodology of comparative legal studies.

Korea's first modern constitution did not address the existence of political parties. The introduction of a constitutional provision on political parties was a response to the growing role of political parties in mass democracy. It is therefore important to analyze the underlying realities of political parties in studying the transplantation of regulations on political parties. In order to grasp the intent behind introducing the constitutional provision on political parties, it also helps to summarize the more general legal regime governing political parties at the time of its introduction. Analyzing both the factual and normative aspects of political parties in Germany and Korea will reveal the differences and similarities in the situations between the place of origin and the target location of the legal provision we are concerned with here.

On this basis, I will examine both the process of introducing Article 21 into the 1949 Basic Law for the Federal Republic of Germany and that of transplanting it into the 1962 Korean Constitution. Furthermore, I will evaluate the appropriateness of the latter measure given the situation prevailing in Korea at the time, and, finally, suggest that there is a need to introduce comparative constitutional law methodology to the socio-legal examination of the transplantation of constitutions.

2. Legal transplantation and comparative legal sociology

This research does not aim to provide an exhaustive account of the methodology of comparative legal studies. Rather, it attempts to compare, at the level of "law in action" rather than just at that of "law in books," the processes by which provisions on political parties made their way into the German and Korean constitutions respectively. As the task of listing, introducing, and discussing different positions on the methodology of comparative law will not fit in with the structure of this text, I will examine only those issues discussed in the realm of comparative law that show a link to the theme of the present work.

implications of this term seem too wide and too general to have any analytical or explanatory power relating to the issues in this field.

2.1 The meaning and methodology of comparative legal studies

The act of comparison is far from seldom done, insofar as it is the starting point of all acts of perception. Except for absolute beings like God, all beings are relative and consequently bound to be perceived by way of comparison. When enacting, interpreting, and studying laws, the impulse to compare the statutory law, legal precedent, and legal theory of different countries or times is completely understandable. The point is rather one about comparing things correctly and properly.

2.1.1 The diversity of comparative legal methods and the need to refine them

Comparative legal studies can be conducted on various levels. Beyond studying another country's law from a domestic perspective, examining different statutes with a view to possible similarities and differences between them, and classifying legal systems into legal families (*Rechtsfamilien*), comparative legal scholars inquiring into the underlying causes of the similarities and differences so perceived may very well come to discover that certain characteristics of a particular legal system have, in fact, been inspired by characteristics of another legal system.

Comparing laws in such diverse ways can be helpful, but at the same time entails certain risks (Watson 1974: 10ff.; Constantinesco 1972: 24ff.). One way of defining comparative studies is as "an act of comparing two or more things and clarifying similarities and differences between them as well as their relations or systems."

Comparative legal studies require an understanding of a multitude of legal systems, that is, of at least one more legal system other than one's own. It is perfectly permissible for such an understanding to be slightly superficial, even substandard, as compared to the kind of understanding required for the in-depth study of a single legal system. At a minimum, however, one may expect accurate knowledge of how a particular legal system taken as a whole has evolved, and how it is related to other systems. Yet it is not easy to understand even an individual area of a foreign legal system. As the scope of study widens, the degree of dependence on secondary sources as opposed to primary ones, as well as the risk of acquiring incorrect information, increases. Besides, it is not easy to establish reasonable criteria when selecting objects of comparison. After having found plausible links between two objects, researchers are tempted to overgeneralize their findings and apply them to other cases that seem similar in appearance.

Discussions on what comparative legal studies consist in, or should be, have the potential to help minimize such risks.

2.1.2 The negative definition of comparative law

As long as it is conducted properly and at various levels, the comparison of legal systems is not to be underestimated. However, its academic value has to be proven if it is to establish itself as an individual discipline in its own right. To that end, comparative law scholars have suggested which types of comparison ought to be excluded from the category of comparative law (Rheinstein 1987: 22ff.; Watson 1974: 4ff.). First, merely studying a foreign legal system in and of itself cannot be enough, even if it were done with an intention to thereby gain a better understanding of one's domestic legal system. Descriptive works, such as those which merely list diverse legal systems or sort them into legal families, must also be ruled out, for they lack the intellectual qualities on which to base an independent academic discipline.

2.1.3 The positive definition of comparative law: The socio-scientific perception of law

A positive definition of comparative law, one that goes beyond a merely negative procedure of ruling out certain kinds of inquiries, is intimately related to the socio-scientific perception of law (Rheinstein 1987: 25ff.). It is grounded in the notion that law, as a means to organize and orient society, is not indifferent to social realities. Understood in this way, legal study means exploring how a legal norm performs its function in a social context. If a law is perceived in terms of its social function, legal studies can criticize the law itself, instead of regarding it as a given needing only to be interpreted or applied. Legal studies are bound to decide which functions legal norms assume in a given society, and whether they perform those functions appropriately. This task can be more satisfactorily achieved by comparing the functioning of a legal norm to that of a norm in another legal system. By exploring the reasons behind the similarities and differences in function, and doing so in a way that is not restricted to just comparing and evaluating a certain number of legal systems, it is possible to simultaneously engage in comparative legal *and* socio-legal analysis.

2.1.4 The object of comparison

The object of comparison must have an attribute of comparability if the comparison is to have any significance. Concerning this attribute, the disciples of the functionalist methodology of comparative law have proposed the term "functional equivalence" (*funktionale Äquivalenz*). Accordingly, comparative legal analysis does not start from a specific legal norm, but instead from a specific social issue, and it involves clarifying what kind of legal means are employed by a certain legal system to address this issue (Rheinstein 1987: 26ff.; Watson 1974: 4ff.; Zweigert and Kötz 1996: 33ff.; Scheiwe 2000: 31ff.). Functional equivalence must be sought across all the various dimensions in which a national legal order functions, not just through a comparison of statutory law. The functionalist approach therefore requires not just exploring legal institutions from an internal perspective, but also analyzing legal effects from an external perspective through the use of socio-legal and socio-scientific means.

The demand that the starting point of the analysis be a social issue rather than a legal norm can be understood as an expression of methodological awareness, more specifically of the desire to take the comparative study of law beyond the mere comparison of norms, with the ultimate aim of establishing comparative law as an independent academic discipline. However, the condition prescribing that the starting point has to be a social issue is overly strict. In reality, it is not rare for a comparative study to start out from a legal norm – as in the case of this study. Once attempts have been made to address a social issue legally, this issue may very well be examined in its new guise as a legal issue.[2]

A position that seeks functional equivalence in social issues is based on the assumption that all industrialized societies have gone through common problems and that, as a result, there is no substantial difference between them.[3] This assumption can be convincing, especially when one compares the norms that regulate economic aspects within the industrialized countries. Nonetheless, a suspicion remains as to whether such an assumption, formulated in relation to civil law, could be applied at all to comparisons between constitutions, which are rather intended to regulate political aspects. This is because the state precedes the industrialization of society, and the political arena is characterized far more by its particularities than is the economy.[4]

The point is to secure objects of comparison in terms that describe the law in action, instead of the law in books, by adding an external perspective to comparative study. According to this assumption, conducting a study in the field of comparative legal sociology is tantamount to finding similar functions among different legal norms, as well as different effects among similar norms.

---

2 For more on the methodology of comparative legal sociology, see Zacher 1977.

3 Rheinstein makes an explicit reference to this issue, see Rheinstein 1987: 26.

4 For more on the problems incurred by functionalist methodology, see Scheiwe 2000: 33ff.

2.1.5 Comparative law and legal history

Every study in the field of legal history has comparative elements. Even when legal historians study the legal institutions of the past, they can hardly escape those of their own times. To avoid superficiality, comparative studies are also obliged to deal with the historical conditions of the legal institutions concerned (Watson 1974: 102ff.; Constantinesco 1972: 51ff.; Zweigert and Kötz 1996: 8). After all, "[h]istory is the element that defines us no less than the present political, economic, or social conditions. Comparative constitutional study is not only about performing horizontal and synchronic comparisons, but also about vertical and diachronic ones" (Choi 1989: 466). Adopting a historical perspective in comparative legal study becomes even more important when studying the transplantation of law.

2.2 The transplantation and assimilation of law

Law is as much formed against the individual background of the community that it regulates as it is disseminated by way of transplantation. Not all the possible cases can be listed exhaustively: Among others, there are cases where a legal system departs from its soil of origin and settles itself in a strange place through various forms of trade, conquest, colonizing, etc., or there are cases where a certain community introduces a foreign legal system for the purpose of regulating its political and social changes.[5] In its early forms, the transplantation of law included the export of laws of ancient Greek city-states to the eastern parts of the Mediterranean, and, later, the spread of Hellenistic culture through the conquests of Alexander the Great. The spread of Roman law through the expansion of the Roman Empire can be taken as a typical example of the transplantation of law in ancient times. In the early modern period, the transplantation of law was also common. Here it pays to note, among other cases, the spread of Roman law, which had been rediscovered in Italian universities, including the University of Bologna, in the Late Middle Ages, throughout the whole of Europe.

2.2.1 Problems of codification and assimilation

To introduce a legal system that has been formed in another community is one thing, but to adapt and assimilate it into a foreign soil so that it can work as

5 Watson emphasizes that while a particular system of positive law expresses a nation's identity, legal transplantation, in which legal norms move around between nations and states, has been universally practiced since the beginning of history. See Watson 1974: 21ff.

intended is quite another.[6] Schwarz has found that not until large-scale codification took place, owing to the conception and consolidation of modern legislative states, did the transplantation of law undergo radical changes (Schwarz 1960: 150ff.). The transplantation of law during the modern era is different to that which transpired beforehand in that it concerns mainly statutory, not customary, law. The modern state, often called the legislative state (*Gesetzgebungsstaat*), succeeded the old state and strengthened state power by concentrating in the monarch political powers which had previously been dispersed in terms of their objects, localities, and functions, and by justifying this in terms of sovereignty, which was said to have legislative power as its main element (Grimm 1986: 61ff.). In their absolutist stage, legislative states tried to improve and partially rationalize existing laws by unifying legislation. After the Enlightenment and the Civil Revolutions, however, the legislative states pursued radically new and unified legislation, tending toward the replacement of the old feudalistic order with a new civil order. The Napoleonic Code of 1804 epitomized the trend. This process of codification was reproduced in Austria, Germany, and Switzerland, among others. And many other countries have in turn transplanted the civil codes of these countries instead of enacting their own, original civil codes.[7]

The opening of the new era of statutory law produced a new problem concerning the transplantation of law (Grimm 1986: 153ff.). Customary laws, which are built up gradually and slowly, can be amalgamated into an established legal system in a subconscious manner, no matter how strange and unfamiliar they are. The transplantation of law by legislation, however, implies a change so radical that it must be branded a "legal revolution" when compared to the transplantation of customary laws, and therefore entails an extremely difficult process of adaptation and assimilation. This difficulty can be mitigated through

---

6 A. B. Schwarz, a scholar of civil law, associates the problem of transplantation of law with that of assimilation. Based on his extraordinary experience as a professor at Istanbul University, Turkey, he analyzed the process of transplanting a Western legal system into a non-Western state and the problems which appear in that process. Turkey adopted the Swiss Civil Code as part of Mustafa Kemal Atatürk's reform program. See Schwarz 1950; 1960.

7 The French Civil Code was transplanted, with little modification, into Belgium, the Netherlands, and Italy, and, with some modifications, into Spain and Portugal. It also influenced the civil codes of Central American, South American, and North African countries. The German Civil Code was transplanted into Hungary, Greece, Russia, Austria, Switzerland, Brazil, and several Northeast Asian countries. See Schwarz 1960: 152.

the customization of foreign statutory law by a legislator in an importing country. As Schwarz points out, however, "it is just a legal code, not the law itself that is imported." While the transplantation of customary laws coincides with their assimilation, the transplantation of statutory laws is only later followed by their assimilation, which does not always produce positive results. The temporal gap between transplantation and assimilation hinders predictions about the effects of assimilation, which can be totally opposite to the intentions of the imported law, not to mention different from its original functions in the exporting country. "Negative assimilation", assimilation which fails to correspond to the intent of transplantation, is the frequent result of such a lack of synchronicity between the transplantation and assimilation of statutory law.

2.2.2 The transplantation of law as a means of modernization

The issue of assimilation becomes critical especially when the law is transplanted as a means of reforming a society in the process of modernization. Under circumstances where a colonial power is enforcing its law on its colonies, or where a country which is lagging behind in the process of modernization decides to accept a legal system that it deems "advanced," it is not rare for the newly introduced statutory law, transplanted without the social institutions that had so far secured its proper functioning, to undergo a process of adaptation to the domestic institutions of its new legal environment.[8] The transplantation of law in the absence of institutions, according to Schwarz, amounts to no more than the transplantation of a legal code. In a true sense, transplantation is carried out along with the formation of conditions enabling the transplanted law to perform its function. This type of transplantation is necessarily accompanied by a long and difficult process of assimilation that will very likely result in negative assimilation as defined above.[9]

---

8 For various examples, see Hooker 1975.

9 The transplantation of the Napoleonic Code into German territorial states is relevant here. While in France the Napoleonic Code preserved and organized the result of the French Revolution, it meant the beginning of a revolutionary social change in Germany. It presupposed a situation in which the feudalistic order, the inherited social class, and the privileges pertaining to the latter had already been abolished, and in which freedom and equality in the modern sense had been brought about. The Kingdom of Westphalia, the model state established in the German territory occupied by Napoleon, did not satisfy these preconditions. This caused some confusion when applying the law, and so the application of some parts of the code came to be reserved. See Grimm 1986: 64ff.

2.2.3 The role of legal notables

The transplantation of statutory law is performed abruptly, without permitting the receiving country enough time to acquire the knowledge of how to apply the transplanted law. As the law tends to take effect even before its assimilation, the transplantation is not a one-off incident, but an unfolding process. If a law is to be assimilated into a new environment, it is necessary to first learn from its country of origin about how to operate it. That is why the transplantation of statutory law is often accompanied by that of legal theory and judicial precedent. In this situation, legal notables (*Rechtshonoratioren*) who understand the legal system of the exporting country come to play an increasingly important role.[10] Schwarz points out that the more complex and unfamiliar the transplanted law, the more likely it is that a group of legal notables will enjoy a nearly monopolistic status (Schwarz 1950: 7).

3. The social and legal background to the German and Korean constitutional provisions on political parties

Before I start analyzing the specifics of the transplantation of Article 21 of the German constitution into the Korean constitution in line with the methodology described above, I would like to compare the structure of the political parties in Germany and in Korea and examine the legal backgrounds to the two countries' respective constitutional provisions on political parties.

3.1 The structure of political parties in Germany and in Korea

3.1.1 Democratic mass-based parties and their transformation into catch-all parties (Volksparteien) *in Germany*

1) Before the Weimar Republic

The parliament of the German Empire was not the place for open discussion about the public interest that it should have been according to the theory of classic parliamentarism. Instead, it became a meeting place for the exchange of opinions and interests between the members of diverse political parties only. Furthermore, these political parties changed into interest parties with the mass organization that occurred at the end of the 19th century. The birth of the Weimar Republic in 1919 meant that political parties gained access to executive power. The introduction of parliamentary democracy in the Weimar

10 On the role of legal notables in legal transplantation, see Rheinstein 1987: 129ff.

Constitution not only gave political parties power to keep the government in check, but also made the government depend on the confidence of a majority of the members of parliament. The rising status of political parties in German constitutional politics was accompanied by a fundamental expansion of the rights of political parties.[11]

2) After World War Two

In Germany, it was important to rebuild the democratic party state that had been demolished by National Socialism. Despite a vacuum of twelve years, the democratic party system was rapidly reconstructed. By 1948, the Social Democratic Party (SPD) – the representative working-class party in Germany – counted 900,000 members in West Germany, and the CDU, with a relatively loose organization, had approximately 400,000 members (Niclauß 1995: 57ff.; 70).

These political parties tried to change the structures of their organization and policies. The birth of the CDU was the starting point of a turn toward developing catch-all parties (*Volksparteien*).[12] The political success of the CDU stimulated the SDP to realign itself and adopt the Godesberg Program in 1959.

3.1.2 Regime parties and notables' parties (Honoratiorenparteien) *in Korea*

The result of the general election of 1950, in which approximately 60 percent of the members of the National Assembly were non-party candidates, shows that the political parties did not play a central role in South Korean politics at that time. The turning point was the founding of the Liberal Party.[13] President Rhee Syngman, without majority support in the National Assembly of 1950, tried to amend the Constitution in order to prolong his rule. To do this, he needed to garner support from outside the National Assembly, and in order to do this founded the Liberal Party. This party soon managed to acquire a nationwide network and millions of members throughout the country by absorbing and mobilizing pre-existing, pro-government interest groups. The first ruling party in Korea thus resulted from top-down mobilization.

In the general election of 1954, the ruling Liberal Party won almost two thirds of the National Assembly seats. The political success of the ruling party stimulated

11 For details, see Song 1996: 118ff.

12 On the formation of catch-all parties in Germany in the postwar period, see Niclauß 1995: 24ff.

13 On the foundation and organization of the Liberal Party in Korea, see Yoon 1990: 278ff; Ahn 1995: 255ff.; National Election Commission 1968: 197ff.

opposition groups to gather into what became the Democratic Party (Kim 1990: 316ff.; Ahn 1995: 261ff.; National Election Commission 1968: 207ff.). However, the Democratic Party was, and remains, a loosely organized elite party.

There was a chance to reform the party system, which at the time consisted only of the dominant ruling party and a loosely organized, weak opposition party, after the democratic revolution of April 1960. However, the chance was lost after the military coup d'état of May 1961.

3.2 The necessity of introducing a constitutional provision on political parties

As mentioned above, there are differences between the political situations and party structures in Germany and in Korea. This fact is reflected in the legislation relating to political parties.

3.2.1 Germany: The collapse of one-party dictatorship and the reconstruction of democracy

The freedom that political parties were guaranteed in the Weimar Republic was revoked under the Hitler regime. After this experience, the notion that democracy cannot be value-neutral became widely accepted in German post-war democracy. On this basis, it was necessary to guarantee, on the one hand, the constitutional status of the freedom of activities of political parties, and, on the other, a means of proper control over their activities.[14]

3.2.2 Korea: Overcoming the authoritarian system through the democratic revolution of April 1960, and the military coup d'état of May 1961

1) Laws on political parties: The US army military government in Korea (USAMGIK) and the Rhee Syngman regime

On November 23rd, 1946, under the then ruling US army military government, a regulation relating to political parties was adopted under the name of

14 A look at EU member states reveals that, next to Germany, France, Greece, Italy, Spain, and Portugal all have constitutional provisions on political parties. The French and Italian constitutions regulate political parties in relation ro party financing and election expenses. Spain and Portugal have separate laws on political parties following the example of Germany. The fact that political parties have no constitutionally guaranteed rights in the UK, Ireland, Holland, Belgium, or Switzerland indicates that the introduction of a constitutional provision on political parties and the experience of total repression of the rights of political parties are mutually related. See Tsatsos et al. 1990.

"USAMGIK decree number 55". It included comprehensive and rigid restraints not only on political parties, but on associations in general. This regulation demanded the registration of associations with three or more members that were in any way related to political activities, and it forbade secret organizations. Furthermore, it demanded that parties submit their member lists and provide details of their activities.

On April 16th, 1952, the second National Assembly was subject to an intervention from the part of the ruling regime at the general election, and so it passed the Law on Political Activities in order to prevent government intervention and protect the freedom of political parties (National Assembly Secretariat 1992: 9064ff.; Song 2000b: 18ff.). This law forbade the direct and indirect intervention of the government and abolished USAMGIK decree number 55.

The Rhee government vetoed this bill and submitted it for reconsideration. While the National Assembly reapproved it in May 1953, the government declined to promulgate the law. In this situation, it insisted that the USAMGIK decree held good, with the result that the latter formed the legal ground of the dissolution of the Progressive Party in 1959.

2) Laws on political parties: The Constitution of 1960

According to the second paragraph of Article 13 of the 1960 Constitution, which was amended on June 15th, 1960, right after the democratic April Revolution, "Political parties are protected by the state, as regulated by laws. However, in case the purposes or activities of a political party are contrary to the fundamental democratic order, the Government can bring an action against that party with the approval of the President, and the Constitutional Court shall rule on the question of its dissolution." Compared with the situation under the Rhee government, when parties could be dissolved by mere administrative decision, this new institution bolstered the constitutional guarantee of political parties (Park 1986: 115).

Moreover, the Law on the Registration of Newspapers and Political Parties of July 1st, 1960, stipulated that political parties register, and that they report the number of their members as well as their activities, financial records, and so on.

The above-mentioned Law on Political Activities was promulgated on October 13th, 1960. Furthermore, the Law on the Constitutional Court, which provided for the dissolution of political parties, was enacted on April 15th, 1961. In this way, the second republic came to be equipped with a relatively balanced set of legal provisions on political parties.

3) The military coup d'état of May 1961

The Military Revolutionary Committee, which came into being with the military coup d'état, forbade all activities of political parties and associations with Proclamation Number 4, and dissolved all of them with Proclamation Number 6. Moreover, a Law on the Purification of Political Activities was passed on March 16th, 1962, which allowed a comprehensive regulation of political activities (National Election Commission 1968: 238). This was the political environment at the time of the birth of the Constitution and the Political Parties Act of 1962.

4. The provision on political parties in the German constitution and its transplantation into the Korean Constitution of 1962

4.1 The genesis of the German constitutional provision on political parties

The German constitutional provision on political parties was introduced in 1949 in the form of Article 21 of the Basic Law for the Federal Republic of Germany. It states that:

(1) Political parties shall participate in the formation of the political will of the people. They may be freely established. Their internal organization must conform to democratic principles. They must publicly account for their assets and for the sources and use of their funds.
(2) Parties that, by reason of their aims or the behavior of their adherents, seek to undermine or abolish the free democratic basic order or to endanger the existence of the Federal Republic of Germany shall be unconstitutional. The Federal Constitutional Court shall rule on the question of unconstitutionality.
(3) Details shall be regulated by federal laws.

4.1.1 The Herrenchiemsee draft constitution

Attempts to introduce provisions on political parties were first made at the Herrenchiemsee convention, which prepared a draft constitution to be submitted to the Parliamentary Council (*Parlamentarischer Rat*). Article 47 of this draft speaks of political parties in relation to the election of the *Bundestag*.

According to this article, only associations submitting themselves to the laws on political parties were able to nominate candidates for election to the *Bundestag*, though this draft did not foresee a purely proportional election system, but instead a mixed one (W. Schreiber 1994: 65).[15] Moreover, Article 47 contained a paragraph aiming to prevent the kind of bloc party system that can, in practice, lead to one-party rule. The exclusive power of political parties to nominate candidates for election to the *Bundestag* was abolished during the debate in the Parliamentary Council.

The experience of Nazi dictatorship and the necessity felt at the time to compete with the one-party system of East Germany formed the background to this regulatory approach.[16]

4.1.2 Discussions in the Parliamentary Council (Parlamentarischer Rat)

While the Parliamentary Council was in charge of making the Basic Law, the Committee on the Organization of the Federal State (*Ausschuss für Organisation des Bundes*) was tasked with deliberating on the provision on political parties. The debate started with Article 47, Paragraph 2, Sentence 2 of the draft, according to which it was prohibited for political parties to enter into agreements with other parties to vote "en bloc." Suhr, who had first suggested this provision, had done so with the aim of preventing one-party rule as seen in the regions occupied by the Soviet Army, not with the aim of preventing parties from forming coalition governments. However, it was broadly taken for granted that a one-party ruling bloc should be banned in a democratic republic, so that any such provision could be declaratory at best (Doemming et al. 1951: 203ff.). Following this discussion, the committee deleted the provision against party blocs.

A more fundamental question about Article 47 was raised in the Committee on the Demarcation of Competences (*Ausschuss für Zuständigkeitsabgrenzung*). Wagner, the chairman of that committee, who doubted the effectiveness of trying to abolish totalitarian parties through party legislation, said, "We cannot subject the genesis and development of political parties to statutory control. There would have been no social democratic party had the Bismarckian regime had laws on political parties." (Werner 1986: 417)

---

15 The first Electoral Law of May 1949 stipulated that 60 per cent of the members of the Bundestag, then consisting of a minimum of 400 members, be elected by plurality voting in single-member districts, while 40 per cent of the seats were to be distributed on the basis of a ratio resulting from the candidates' respective performances in their local constituencies. See Schreiber 1994: 65.

16 O. Suhr and H. J. Brill, who experienced the political situation in the Soviet Zone, are known to have played important roles in introducing Article 47 into the Herrenchiemsee Draft. See Hennis 1992: 27.

The provision on political parties was afterwards moved from the section on elections to the section on general state power (Parlamentarischer Rat 1948/49: 48; Doemming et al. 1951: 205). It was finalized following discussions in the Main Committee (*Hauptausschuss*) and in the Plenary.

4.1.3 Evaluation

The draft of the provision on political parties mainly contained regulations that reflected the drafters' attempts to excuse themselves for their impotence in the face of the Nazi regime and of one-party rule in the Soviet Zone. However, the voices which focused on the basic principle of the right to form political parties were unremitting, and the provisions of the draft were revised accordingly in the Parliamentary Council.

This shows that constitutional rationality functioned well, despite the tricky situation. The main rationale given here was that the means for controlling a democratic party system should not lead to a limitation of political life.[17]

4.2 The introduction of the provision on political parties into the Constitution of 1962

Article 7 of the 1962 Constitution introduced the provision on political parties as follows:

(1) The establishment of political parties shall be free, and the plural party system shall be guaranteed.
(2) Political parties shall be democratic in their organization, and activities, and shall have the necessary organizational arrangements for the people to participate in the formation of the political will.
(3) Political parties shall enjoy the protection of the State. If the purposes or activities of a political party are contrary to the fundamental democratic order, the Government may bring an action against it in the Supreme Court for its dissolution, and the political party shall be dissolved in accordance with the decision of the Supreme Court.

This is not really different from Article 21 of the Basic Law, with the exception of the duty to disclose party financing. However, the 1962 Constitution states, in addition, that candidates for general or presidential elections must be nominated by political parties (Article 36, Paragraph 3; Article 64, Paragraph 3). This means that it prevented independents from standing at elections. Furthermore,

17 See the statement of SDP Congressman Menzel. See Werner 1986: 521ff.; especially 523.

Article 38 of the Constitution states that "if a member of the National Assembly changes or withdraws from his party (except merging and expulsion), or if his party is dissolved, he shall lose his seat."[18] This article placed extreme emphasis on being tied to a party, and, in reality, on the monopoly of the political parties over politics (Kwon 1998: 95).[19]

Moreover, the Political Parties Act was passed in December 1962. This Act laid down rigid requirements for the founding of political parties. It stipulated that parties must have party chapters in one third or more of all electoral districts, and that each electoral district chapter must have 50 or more members. It also disqualified civil servants, board members of public or state-owned enterprises, teachers, and journalists from joining political parties.

The following details the birth process of the provision on political parties in relation to constitutional theories.

4.2.1 The process of constitution making[20]

Park Chung-Hee, the chairman of the Supreme State-Rebuilding Committee, declared on August 12th, 1961, that political parties would be allowed to be active from the beginning of 1963, and that a new constitution would be made before March of the same year. He also mentioned the basic elements of this new constitution, which was to include a presidential system, a unicameral legislature, and publicly managed elections (Park 1963: 66f.; National Election Commission 1968: 238; Lee 2000: 126).

On this basis, the Constitutional Committee was founded in July 1962.[21] There were 8 chief members and 21 experts, including scholars of law, politics,

---

18 According to Professor Han Tae-Yeon, there was a strong opinion that a member of the National Assembly should lose his seat in case of expulsion from his party. See Han 1998.

19 Professor Kwon Yeong-Seong calls this "an extreme party state." See Kwon 1998: 95.

20 In preparing for the 1962 Constitution, there was some discussion about whether what was at issue was making a new constitution or simply amending the existing one. The Supreme State-Rebuilding Committee decided to use the expression "constitutional amendment", on the grounds that "making a new constitution could cause trouble for the country's identity in international relations" (Ministry of Public Information 1962: 16), and the process officially became known as "the constitutional amendment." However, as the procedural and the substantive aspects of this process had strong characteristics of constitution making, it will be called "constitution making" here.

21 On the process of making the 1962 Constitution, see Ministry of Public Information 1962: 67ff.; Seo 1986: 232ff.; Song 1980: 197ff.; Lee 2000: 126ff.

and economics. The committee had its first meeting on July 16th, and organized a sub-committee with 9, mainly constitutional, legal scholars. The sub-committee discussed the draft of the constitution and some American experts participated in the final stage of the discussions.[22]

The Supreme State-Rebuilding Committee approved the bill for a new constitution on November 3rd, but proposed and announced it on November 5th. On December 6th, the Supreme Committee put the bill to a vote and it was passed unanimously. This bill was put to a referendum on December 17th in accordance with the Referendum Act, and was approved with 78 percent of the votes.

4.2.2 Discussions on the provision on political parties

The sub-committee included the provision on political parties in its list of twelve main issues to be submitted to the Constitutional Committee. But the following discussion focused on (1) whether to have a presidential or a parliamentary system; (2) whether to have a unicameral or bicameral legislature; (3) the contents of and protection of fundamental rights; (4) whether to establish a constitutional court; and (5) whether what was at issue was constitution making or constitutional amendment. The discussion did not deal with the provision on political parties.

But if we read between the lines of the discussion, we see that a preference had already been expressed for a strong party state. The only problem was how to reflect this in the constitutional text. The Constitutional Committee, preparing for a public hearing, discussed "whether to introduce the provision on political parties into the constitution, and, if so, how to apply it (with a view to organizations, assets etc.) to prevent the recurrence of previous problems and to build healthy political parties." (Ministry of Public Information 1962: 538ff.) The committee's statement that "there is no need for a public hearing on the inclusion of a provision regulating the internal democracy of political parties and the financing of political parties since there will be no opposition to such a provision" shows that Article 7 of the 1962 Constitution was not a concern, and that the introduction of Article 36, Paragraph 3, of Article 64, Paragraph 3, and of Article 38, which guaranteed party monopoly, had already been decided irrespective of public opinion.

The hearing held by the Constitutional Committee discussed the provision on political parties at length. Professor Gal Bong-guen, who represented the Korean

22 On the advice given by Professors Emerson and Flanz in the process of making the 1962 Constitution, see Lee 2000: 129ff.

Public Law Association, approved of the provision and focused on the need for parties to disclose their financing.[23] He also insisted on prohibiting independents from running for election (National Assembly of the Republic of Korea 1967: 16ff.). The speakers of other groups expressed similar opinions. Most of them seemed to have been mobilized by the state for its own purposes.

This extreme version of the party state was not discussed in the Constitutional Committee until August 7th, 1962. However, it can be presumed that the ban on independent candidates, as well as the rule about losing one's seat in the case of a change in party membership, had already been decided by the regime. In this regard, it is worth noting that constitution-making processes were already underway before the establishment of the Constitutional Committee (Ministry of Public Information 1962: 67), and that there existed another draft constitution made by the KCIA (Korea Central Intelligence Agency). According to the testimony of Professor Han Tae-yeon, the original draft constitution was prepared by the KCIA, and the Political Parties Act was drafted by the Legislation and Judiciary Committee, a subordinate committee of the Supreme Council for National Reconstruction. This claim is also made in the autobiography of Lee Suk-je, who was the chairman of the Legislation and Judiciary Committee and the person in charge of all work related to the constitution-making process (Lee 1995: 179).

The fact that preparations were made to found the ruling Republican Party in summer 1962 under the leadership of KCIA executive Kim Jong-pil (Kim 1984: 161), combined with the fact that the KCIA had submitted its own draft constitution and that the scholars who participated in drafting that constitution were also part of the Committee, suggests that the constitutional provision on political parties reflects these protagonists' aim of mobilizing their party and driving the "modernization of the fatherland."

4.2.3 *Theoretical background*

It would be helpful to look at the general trend in constitutional theory on political parties at the time, as representative constitutional law scholars also participated in the constitution-making process.

Before the April Revolution, Professor Han Tae-yeon explained in his paper "Constitution and Political Parties" that democratic states tend to be party states in which political parties are regarded as a kind of "intermediate power." (Han 1959: 145–149) He argued that the freedom of political parties should be

23 However, the article about party financing was not included in the Constitution.

protected by the freedom of speech, press, assembly, and association, and by a "free democratic political order" as an immanent principle of the constitution.

It is noteworthy that debates on political parties were intense right after the military coup d'état, when the discussion on the new constitution arose. Professor Park Il-kyung insisted that the freedom of political parties, the parties' vocation not to be mere interest groups, their internal democracy, their public financing, and the possibility of their dissolution by judicial power should be stipulated by the constitution, and that two or three main parties should be promoted in order to prevent minor parties from overrunning the scene, even though that is not a matter for constitutional law (Park 1962: 91ff.). The need to prohibit the changing of party membership was also mentioned (Mun 1962: 19). Additionally, foreign examples of Political Parties Acts in Argentina (Park 1962: 86ff.), in Germany (Kim 1962: 18–43), and in other countries were also referred to.

As discussions continued about constitutional theories, Carl Schmitt's theories of parliamentary crisis and of democratic identity, as well as Leibholz's theory of the "party state" (*Parteienstaat*), were also introduced into the debate (see Mun 1962: 16–19). These theories, which differentiate the party state principle based on democracy from the parliamentary principle based on liberalism, had the potential to legitimize an authoritarian party state model. Another noteworthy aspect concerns the fact that discussions did not fully take into account the differing realities of party politics in Korea and in Germany.

Although Leibholz's theory did not become dominant at that time, the emphasis on the party state formed the general trend. However, there was, at least, no extreme position to be found in the literature advocating that political parties be granted a monopoly on politics.

4.2.4 *Evaluation*

The political slogan of the military regime was "modernization of the fatherland." In order to modernize politics, political parties were to be modernized so that they could be "engines" working to accelerate political modernization (Baek 1962: 16).

In reality, however, the new legal norms comprehensively limited the rights and freedoms of political parties. Indeed, the aim in introducing a provision on "political parties" from a developed country was merely to justify the establishment of an authoritarian and exclusive legal system. In order to lend credibility to the pretext that the legal reforms establishing such a system were modernizing reforms, a large number of constitutional law scholars and intellectuals were persuaded, or indeed forced, to take part in them. Moreover, Leibholz's theory of the party state was applied in an authoritarian way. The leaders of the military coup d'état founded a new ruling party named the Republican Party. This was a typical mass party whose members comprised more than ten percent of all eligible voters.[24]

5. Concluding remarks

At the start of this essay, I emphasized some methodological considerations for research in comparative law. I argued that it does not seem possible to apply a rigid comparative methodology to each and every situation. There should be greater methodological flexibility in cases where a scholar from a specific legal area undertakes comparative research. However, this cannot legitimize an ignorance of methodological considerations. Given the speed of social and technological change, and the scope of international exchanges, modern countries share more and more common problems. This is why there is both an increased opportunity and an increased need for legal transplantation in modern society, as well as an increased risk of inappropriate transplantations.

In this paper, I have analyzed the transplantation of the German constitutional provision on political parties, Article 21 of the Basic Law, into the Korean Constitution within a comparative socio-legal framework. Reflecting the Nazi experience and that of the beginning of the Cold War in Germany, the provision on political parties originally introduced in Article 47 of the Herrenchiemsee draft was highly regulative, but was then mitigated after a discussion in the Parliamentary Council for its insertion into the Basic Law as Article 21. In the Korean case, a relatively balanced provision on political parties was introduced into the Constitution in 1960, following the experience of political parties being suppressed under the Rhee Syngman regime. Article 7 of the 1962 Constitution, a direct import of Article 21 of the Basic Law, amounted to nothing more than a gloss on other provisions in the Constitution and the Political Parties Act that were contrary to the rationale of constitutionalism. While Article 7 of the Constitution was celebrated as being a modern constitutional provision befitting a developed country, provisions which enabled party monopoly in elections, excessive party discipline, and a rigid regulation of political activity were

24 When the Republican Party was founded on the 27th of February 1962, it had 138,131 members. The number had increased dramatically by the time of the presidential elections on the 15th of October 1962 to 1,568,006, and in 1967 there were over 1,700,000 members amounting to 12.1 percent of all eligible voters. See Kim 1996: 133ff.

introduced through the back door. The legal vestiges of these provisions remain today, and so Korean society still needs to reform the laws regulating politics if it is to allow full freedom of political activities.

The provision on political parties of the 1962 Constitution is an example of negative assimilation – assimilation which fails to correspond to the intent of transplantation – undertaken in the name of modernization. This does not, however, rule out the possibility that the provision on political parties of the present Korean constitution might very well still come to unfold its full normative potential.

References

Ahn, Cheol-hyun. 1995. "Che 1–2 konghwaguk chŏngdang chŏngch'i-ŭi chŏn'gae kwajŏng-kwa t'ŭksŏng [The Development and the Characteristics of Party Politics under the Rhee, Syngman regime and the 1960 Constitution]." In *Hanguk chŏngdang chŏngch'iron [Studies on Party Politics in Korea],* edited by Ahn, Hee-Soo. Seoul: Nanam, 253–284.

Bae, Byung-sam. 2003. "Han'guk chŏngch'ihak-ŭi kiwon-kwa chŏngch'esŏng t'amsaek [In search for the origins and identity of Korean political science]." *Han'gukjŏngch'ihakhoebo [Journal of the Korean Association for Political Science],* Vol. 73, No. 2. 87–105.

Baek, Sang-geon. 1962. "Chŏngch'i-ŭi kŭndaehwa [Modernization of Politics]." *Pŏbjewŏlbo [Monthly Legislation Review],* December. 7–17.

Choi, Dai-kwon. 1989. *Hŏnbŏphak – Pŏbsahoehakjŏk Chŏpgŭn [Constitutional Law – A Legal Sociological Approach].* Seoul: Pagyŏngsa.

Constantinesco, Léontin Jean. 1972. *Rechtsvergleichung* Bd. II. Cologne: Heymann.

Constitutional Court of the Republic of Korea. 2006. "*Chŏngdangbŏp che-25-cho tŭng-ŭi wihŏnsŏng-e taehan kyŏlchŏng*" [Judgment on the unconstitutionality of Article 25 etc. of the Political Parties Act]. *Hŏnbŏpchaep'anso kyŏlchŏngmun* [18 Constitutional Court Decision Collection]. 402–416.

Czarniawska, Barbara, and B. Joerges. 1996. "Travels of ideas." In *Translating Organizational Change,* edited by B. Czarniawska and G. Sevon. Berlin: Walter de Gruyter, 13–48.

Doemming, Klaus-Berto, Füsslein, Rudolf Werner, und Werner Matz. 1951. "Entstehungsgeschichte der Artikel des Grundgesetzes" *AöR.*

Evans, Peter. 2003. "Development as Institutional Change: The Pitfalls of Monocropping and the Potentials of Deliberation." *Studies in Comparative International Development,* Vol. 38, 30–52.

Grimm, Dieter. 1986. "Historische Erfahrung mit Rechtsvergleichung – das frühe 19. Jahrhundert in Deutschland." *Rabels Zeitschrift für ausländisches und internationales Privatrecht,* Vol. 50, 61–76.

Han, Tae-Yeon. 1959. "*Hŏnbŏp-gwa chŏngdang* [Constitutional Law and Political Parties]" *The Goshigye* June. 145–149.

Han, Tae-Yeon. 1998. "Minjujuŭi-wa chŏngdang kukka II [Democracy and party states II)" *Koshi Yŏn'gu (Study for the National Bar Examination),* Vol. 25, Vol. 2. 102–115.

Hennis, Wilhelm. 1992. „"Der 'Parteienstaat' des Grundgesetzes." In *Die Kontroverse Weizsäckers Parteienkritik in der Diskussion,* edited by Gunter Hofmann and Werner A. Perger. Frankfurt: Eichborn, 25–50.

Hooker, Barry. 1975. *Legal Pluralism*. Oxford: Clarendon Press.

Kim, Tae-Il. 1990. "Minjudang-ŭi sŏngkyŏk-kwa yŏkhal [The Characteristics and the Role of the Democratic Party]." In *Han'guk chŏnch'iron I [Study on Korean Politics I]*, edited by Bae-Ho Han. Seoul: Nanam, 311–342.

Kim, Jeong-Won. 1984. "Kunjŏng-gwa che 3 konghwa'guk: 1961–1971 [Military Government and the 3rd Republic: 1961–1971]" In *Nyŏndae [The 1960's],* edited by Kim, Seong-Hwan et al. Seoul: Kŏrŭm, 150–207.

Kim, Kyeong-Jae. 1962. "Sŏdokŭi chŏngdang-gwa sŏn'gŏ [Political Parties and Elections in West Germany]" *Pŏbjewŏlbo [Monthly Legislation Review],* December. 18–43.

Kwon, Yeong-Seong. 1998. *Hŏnbŏphak wŏnron [Study on Constitutional Law].* Seoul: Bomunsa.

Kim, Yong-Wook. 1996. "Minju konghwadang-ŭi uisang-gwa tangjŏng kwan'gye [The Status of the Republican Party and the Government-Ruling Party Relationship]" In *Han'guk hyŏndae chŏngch'iron II [Study on Korean Modern Politics II],* edited by Bae-Ho Han. Seoul: Nanam, 109–159.

Lee, Suk-Je. 1995. *Kakha, uri hyŏkmyŏng hapshida* [Let's Begin a Revolution]. Seoul: Sŏjŏkp'o.

Lee, Wan-Beom. 2000. "Che 3 konghwaguk hŏnbŏp chejŏng kwajŏng-gwa kŭ sŏnggyŏk: 'Minjŏng Yiyang' kwa 'kangryŏkhan taet'ongryŏngje. [The Making of the 1962 Constitution and its Characteristics: A 'Transfer of Power to Civil Government' and a 'Strong Presidental System']" Paper presented at the Symposium on Korean Constitutional History, Korean Association for Political and Diplomatic History/Social Science Research Institute, Konkuk University, Seoul, February 125–145, 2000

The Research Bureau, Ministry of Public Information. 1962. *Hŏnbŏp kaejŏng-gwa kukmin t'u'p'yo [Constitutional Amendment and Referendum].* Seoul: Kongbobu.

Mun, Hong-Ju. 1962. "Sae ŭihoe chedo-ŭi mosŭp [A Sketch of the New Parliamentary System]" *Pŏbjŏng* (Law and Politics) July. 16–19.

National Assembly of the Republic of Korea. 1967. *Hŏnbŏp kaejŏng shimwirok* [Deliberation on the Constitutional Amendment], Vol. 2. Seoul.

National Assembly Secretariat. 1992. *Taehanmin'guk pŏbryul'an yŏnhyŏkjip [The History of Legislative Bills of the Republic of Korea],* Vol. 9. Seoul.

National Election Commission. 1968. *Taehanmin'guk chŏngdangsa [History of Korean Political Parties]. Seoul.*

Niclauß, Karlheinz. 1995. *Das Parteiensystem der Bundesrepublik Deutschland. Paderborn:* UTB.

Park, Chung-hee. 1963. "Jeonggwon yiyang Shigi e gwanhan seongmyeong [Statement on the Time of the Transfer of Power]," 12.8.1961, the Compilation Committee for the History of Korean Military Revolution, the Supreme State-Rebuilding Committee, *Hanguk gunsa hyeokmyeongsa* [The History of Korean Military Revolution], Vol. 2 No. 2, Seoul, 1963.

Park, Il-Gyeong. 1962. "Shinsaeng konghwa'guk-gwa chŏngdang [A New Republic and Political Parties]" *The Goshigye* June. 83–92.

Park, Il-Gyeong. 1986. *Shin hŏnbophak wŏnron [A New Study on Constitutional Law].* Seoul: Pŏpkyŏng Ch'ulpănsa.

Parlamentarischer Rat. 1948/49. *Verhandlungen des Hauptausschusses.* Bonn: Bonner Universitäts-Buchdruckerei Gebr. Scheur.

Perju, Vlad. 2012. "Constitutional Transplants, Borrowing, and Migrations." In *The Oxford Handbook of Comparative Constitutional Law*, edited by Michel Rosenfeld and András Sajó. Oxford: Oxford University Press, 1304–1327.

Scheiwe, Kirsten. 2000. „Was ist ein funktionales Äquivalent in der Rechtsvergleichung?" *Kritische Vierteljahresschrift für Gesetzgebung und Rechtswissenschaft* 83. Jg. 30–51.

Schreiber, Wolfgang. 1994. *Handbuch des Wahlrechts zum Deutschen Bundestag* 5th ed. Cologne: Heymanns.

Schwarz, Andreas B. 1950. *Das Schweizerische Zivilgesetzbuch in der ausländischen Rechtsentwicklung.* Zürich: Schulthess.

Schwarz, Andreas B. 1960. "Rezeption und Assimilation ausländischer Rechte." In *Rechtsgeschichte und Gegenwart,* edited by Andreas Bertalan Schwarz, Hans Thieme and Franz Wieacker. Karlsruhe: Müller.

Seo, Byeong-Jo. 1986. *Kaehon shibi [An Argument over Constitutional Amendment]*. Seoul: Hyŏndae Munyesa.

Song, Seog-Yun. 1996. *Politische Parteien und Verbände in der Verfassungsrechtslehre der Weimarer Republik*. Berlin: Duncker & Humblot.

Song, Seog-Yun. 2000a. "The Party Clause of the German Constitution and its Transplantation to Korea: A Comparative Socio-Legal Approach." *Seoul Law Journal* 41.3. 115–146.

Song, Seog-Yun. 2000b. "Chŏngch'i ch'egye-ŭi sinjindaesa-wa chŏngch'i kwan'gyebŏp [The Metabolism of Political Systems and Laws on Politics]" *Democratic Legal Studies* 17. 13–42.

Song, Woo. 1980. *Han'guk hŏnbŏp kaejŏngsa [The History of Constitutional Amendment in Korea]*. Seoul: Jipmoon.

Tsatsos, Dimitris, Dian, Schefold and Hans-Peter Schneider. 1990. *Parteienrecht im Europäischen Vergleich*. Baden-Baden: Nomos.

Watson, Alan. 1974. *Legal Transplants – An Approach to Comparative Law*. Edinburgh: Scottish Academic Press.

Werner, Wolfram. 1986. "Ausschuß für Zuständigkeitsabgrenzung." In *Vol. 3 Der Parlamentarische Rat 1948–1949. Akten und Protokolle,* edited by Deutscher Bundestag und Bundesarchiv. Boppard am Rhein: Boldt.

Yoon, Yong-Hee. 1990. "Chayudang-ŭi kigu-wa yŏkhal [The Organization and the Role of the Liberal Party]." In *Han'guk chŏngch'iron I* [Studies on Korean Politics I], edited by Bae-Ho Han. Seoul: Nanam, 277–310.

Zacher, Hans F. 1977. "Vorfragen zu den Methoden der Sozialrechtsvergleichung." In *Methodische Probleme des Sozialrechtsvergleichs,* edited by H.F. Zacher. Berlin: Duncker & Humblot, 21–74.

Zweigert, Konrad and Hein Kötz. 1996. *Einführung in die Rechtsvergleichung* (3rd ed.). Tübingen: Mohr Siebeck.

Hannes B. Mosler

(6) Legal Translations "Made In Korea"

> [W]hat we can see more clearly [...] is that in this process of translation there is always gain and always loss, always transformation; that the "original meaning" of the text cannot be our meaning, for restating it in our terms, in our world, no matter how faithfully or literally, we produce something new and different (White 1990: 241).

> In building the new [legal] tradition, we cannot simply copy or borrow. Our experiment will be uniquely our own, whether we desire it to be so or not (Hahm 1971: 83).

Abstract The author applies the analytical concept of *translation* to the generation and alteration of legal ideas and norms in Korea, whereby the Korean constitution and its provision on political parties, together with other Korean laws related to political parties, serve him as representative cases.

1. Introduction

South Korea (hereafter: Korea) is typical of countries that are said to have borrowed or adopted substantial parts of their legal ideas, norms, and practices from "developed countries." Earlier kingdoms and dynasties of Korea had close relations with those of China for many centuries. Korea later endured foreign occupation by the Japanese empire for about half a century, and for decades afterwards was a so-called developing country under strong U.S. influence. Not surprisingly, the influence of these countries has also made itself felt in the area of Korean law. One of the most central and lasting influences on Korea's legal culture, however, can be traced back to the German legal tradition. The encounter between the two legal systems at first did not take the form of direct contact, but instead was mediated by Japanese occupation. The lasting influence of German legal culture can be put down to several factors, one of which is that it was introduced by colonial masters at a point of time when Korea was still in its adolescence, that is, still in the formative stages of its "modernization." This gives us an interesting and potentially promising viewpoint from which to examine the manner in which legal ideas travel across borders. Doing so will help us understand the process of epistemic circulation.

In the area of constitutional law, and of law on political parties in particular, Korean legal scholars and judges often refer to German law and scholarship to back up their positions on, or interpretations of, specific statutes and cases. However, it is striking that this frequent practice is not based on any kind of explicit, systematic statement of reasons. In other words, no substantial explanation is given as to why German law can be drawn upon to support certain interpretations, and why such reference should carry any authoritative weight.[1] Textbooks and seminal works in the field of legal studies introduce, discuss, and analyze German law and legal traditions, but they are mostly silent about the grounds for this assumed compatibility and validity. Indeed, there seems to be a tacit agreement that German law and scholarship may be referred to as a standard of judgment. Another astonishing fact is that in spite of the fact that German law and legal texts are held in high regard – some Korean laws are obviously closely modeled on German laws – Korean provisions inspired by German law tend to lack in practical impact. In addition, technocratic tinkering brings about frequent top-down legal reform, commonly in the name of the rule of law (*Rechtsstaatlichkeit*) and political progress, which then leads to a gap between constitutional law and constitutional reality. As I will attempt to show in the empirical analysis supplied below, the Korean constitution and its provision on political parties, as well as other legal provisions related to political parties, count among the most prominent examples in this respect.

Different perspectives may be brought to bear on this gap between constitutional law and constitutional reality. Some might argue that the problem here can be put down to "the national soul being in the wrong legal body," thus emphasizing the uniqueness of Korean identity and its incompatibility with norms and ideas stemming from different contexts. Others, who are more technically minded, might describe the gap as a case of "pre-modern antibodies fighting modern transplants," or of the "soil being poor in the kinds of mineral nutrients needed by delicate transplants," thereby at once indicating ways to bridge the very gaps they identified. In this chapter, I aim to conceptualize and analyze the phenomenon of the circulation of legal ideas and norms from the perspective of *translation*. Seen from this angle, it is possible to explain the gap between constitutional law and constitutional reality as a case of "losses and gains in translation" – or as the result of creativity in the making of legal ideas and norms.[2]

---

1 Of course, there is abundant literature dealing with the historical developments that lead to the resemblance of Korean and German law in a descriptive fashion. See for example Choi (1981), Huh (1977) or Kim (1985; 2003).

2 By "losses and gains" I do not mean "mistranslations." That would imply that there is such a thing as a "correct" translation of an "original," something the translation perspective, as I advocate it here, denies. Instead, I take "losses and gains" to mean that the original is lost and that something new is gained in the process of drawing on foreign legal ideas and norms. Put differently, translations are authentic creations referencing other norms and ideas (or their translations). The concept of translation is elaborated in more detail below.

My epistemological interest is threefold. First, I intend to contribute theoretically to the development of a translational approach through critical research on the circulation of legal ideas and norms (e.g. Song 2000; 2012; Örücü 2002; Evans 2003; Langer 2004; Rehm 2008). To do so, I borrow from the literature on policy translation (Freeman 2006; 2009; Johnson and Hagström 2005) as well as from existing legal translation literature (Langer 2004). Second, I aim to both demonstrate the superior explanatory power of the translation approach as a metaphorical device when compared to the transplantation perspective, and to showcase it as a workable methodology. Third, by applying this approach to an empirical case, I want to provide new insights into specific instances of legal change and their political implications for Korea.

In section two below, I begin by offering a theoretical account of the metaphor of *legal transplantation* as it is broadly used in legal scholarship, together with an illustration of its practical application. On the basis of this discussion, I then juxtapose this perspective of *legal transplantation* with that of *legal translation* as a heuristic device for explaining the circulation of legal ideas. In section three, I utilize the metaphorical concept of *translation* for an operational method for empirical analysis. Then, in section four, I demonstrate the advantages of the legal translation approach and its method by applying it to a representative case. Finally, I conclude by summarizing the findings and explaining their implications.

2. From legal trans*plantation* to legal *translation*

One of the most widely cited metaphorical devices for capturing the circulatory movements of legal ideas and norms is that of "transplantation," a usage that Watson (1974) and Kahn-Freund (1974) explicitly endorse. Watson's notion of "legal transplant" (Watson 1974) in particular is cited in the work of two scholars as a way of providing an indicatory basis of their theoretical approach to the phenomenon. The first, Rehm (2008), deals with the rather abstract question of the feasibility of using legal transplants as instruments for successful law reform. The second, Song (2000), scrutinizes an actual occurrence of "legal transplantation" from Germany to Korea as a representative case of political modernization in developing countries through the adoption of constitutional norms from "the West." While the former tackles the theme in a way that is more concerned with theory building, the latter approaches the field in a more empirical fashion. Both, however, share a similar epistemological interest, namely the desire to depart from existing conceptions in the legal studies literature, which either denounce the importance of domestic characteristics or claim that law and legal norms cannot be transferred at all. Rehm and Song do this by referring to sociological and political scientific perspectives, but also have their own research agendas as jurists. This leads them to provide insightful analyses and findings which constitute the starting point of my endeavor. From my post-positivistic ontological perspective of "translation," I find various aspects of their propositions useful to constructive examination. Against this backdrop, I attempt, from a political science perspective, to contribute to developing an approach that allows us to grasp the complexity of processes of circulation of legal norms and ideas.

What I shall do in the following paragraphs, without in the least wanting to underrate Rehm's and Song's works as pieces of research in their own right, is to engage in a critical dialogue with these two scholars' elaborations on transplantation as an opportunity to show both the theoretical and practical advantages of the analytical approach of *legal translation*.[3] In a manner comparable to scholarly efforts in the literature on *policy translation* attempting to dissociate policy translation from the dominant discourse replete with conceptions such as "transfer," "diffusion," or "learning", I try to revamp the metaphorical expression "legal transplant" and use it as a *heuristic device* for "legal translation."

2.1 Legal transplantation in theory

Against the backdrop of the needs and experiences of transitional countries, Rehm (2008) begins his inquiry with the question of whether the strategy of legal transplantation can be successful – theoretically as well practically – and, if so, under what conditions they are to be recommended as tools for legal reform (Rehm 2008: 2).[4] His metaphorical vocabulary goes back mainly to Alan Watson (1974) and Otto Kahn-Freund (1974), who are generally credited with having coined the transplantation metaphor in the context of law and comparative legal research. Watson in particular is considered a forerunner in the field on the ground of proposing that the most fruitful legal change would be legal borrowing, or transplanting. This "Watson thesis" can be divided into a "strong" and a "weak" variant (Ewald 1995: 489), or into a "strong" and a "weak" "transplantation thesis." The strong thesis

3 I am clearly aware of the fact that at least half of the following critical examination might come under attack for seeming to set up a mere straw man, since Rehm and Song each pursued a set of aims in writing their texts that differs from the agenda of this contribution. But this kind of "shadow boxing", I submit, will still prove helpful in trying to distil the advantages of the translation metaphor and advance the research agendas of related strands of inquiry.

4 This question is similar but ultimately different to Eun-Jeung Lee's question about the conditions required for a successful transfer of knowledge (see Lee's contribution in this volume).

posits that all legal transformations have to be understood as the result of legal transplantations, while the weak variant assumes that only major legal transformations refer back to transplantations (Rehm 2008: 11). The transplantation thesis is essentially an attempt to counter the strong variant of the "mirror theory." This theory contends that law and legal norms are exclusively determined by economic, social, and cultural factors (Rehm 2008: 17). In other words, insofar as law is determined by factors such as relations of production (Marx), geography, climate, and national identity (Montesquieu), and/or nation-specific cultural socialization (Legrand), it can neither "travel" nor be "transplanted," since it is nothing but a mirror image of the respective national legal system. The weak "mirror theory" proposed by Ewald (1995) accepts the existence of some endogenous factors able to influence the respective national "container," as well as the exogenous determination of law due to transfers (see Table 1). Rehm (2008), as for him, seems to opt for a weak transplantation thesis insofar as he answers his opening question about successful transplantations with a "yes, but." According to him, legal transplantation can indeed be a tool for the reform of legal systems in transitional countries, provided the transplant is thoroughly examined with a view to its compatibility. This sounds like a circular argument, but it actually is not. Let me explain why by illustrating how the author uses the term "transplantation."

Table 1: Comparison of "mirror theses" and "transplantation theses"

	Mirror thesis	**Transplantation thesis**
Strong	Legal norms cannot be transplanted	All legal transformations are transplants
Weak	Transplantation is possible in parts	Only major legal transformations are transplants

Rehm (2008) states that transplantations "cannot be performed through schematic and mechanic one-to-one transfers, but have to take into account the conditions of the receiving country" (Rehm 2008: 39; my translation). Transplantation would have to be "designed in such a way that it is capable of developing further in the future" (Rehm 2008: 39; my translation). It ought not to involve the "blind adoption of a legal system for political reasons" or the "crafting of a suitable compromise modeled on a large number of different legal systems" (Rehm 2008: 39; my translation). Rather, transplantation should be carried out through a "search for a solution that is suitable for the specific economic, cultural, but also legal cultural and linguistic needs of a country" (Rehm 2008: 39; my translation). The author maintains that "[l]aw will stay a dead letter if no attempt is made to anchor it in the heads and decisions of those concerned, that is, in legal reality" (Rehm 2008: 40; my translation). He also stresses that "legal transplants should be considered and, if necessary, implemented with great care and in close consultation with representatives of a foreign legal order" (Rehm 2008: 41). Law and legal norms can only exist when embedded in a concrete linguistic, political, economic, and social environment (Rehm 2008: 41; my translation). Only thus deployed can transplants prove to be of any assistance (Rehm 2008: 32).

It is interesting to note that in trying to demonstrate the possibilities and capabilities of transplants as tools of legal reform, the author, for the most part, has to qualify his explanations to such a degree that the argument in favor of using the transplantation metaphor becomes increasingly indistinct and, at times, even appears altogether unwarranted. This would seem to be due to the shortcomings of the expression in this particular context. Followed through rigorously, the logic of the "transplantation" approach suggests that a law performs identical functions in the "donor" and in the "recipient" country; that legal norms are empty containers with only one permanently assigned function respectively; that legal norms are transplanted as a whole; that laws are implanted into previously entirely self-contained organisms; and that there is somebody who performs the operation of transplanting the norm, just like an organ, from one place to another. However, this is not what happens in reality, which is why Rehm has to qualify the transplantation metaphor every time he argues against the strong mirror and the strong transplantation theory in order to find an appropriate common ground on which to make his point (see, for example, Rehm 2008: 39). In fact, the legal transfers he sets out to examine are far too sophisticated in nature for the transplantation metaphor to be able to capture them. To give an example, Rehm maintains that "legal systems [...] communicate with each other" (Rehm 2008: 8; my translation), when "communication" cannot, in truth, be expressed in terms of "transplantation."

This difficulty, it seems to me, originates in the transplantation metaphor itself, which is simply not capable of translating the full range of dynamics and interactions in legal transfer processes into a workable notion for the purposes of description, let alone analysis. Langer (2004) illustrates these metaphorical pitfalls well in pointing out the main shortcomings of the transplantation allegory (Langer 2004: 30–32). First of all, it fails to account for the possibility of transferring legal norms only in part, or only on specific levels, in that one cannot trans*plant* the heart's left atrium or a flower's blossom in isolation and assume that everything will "work out just fine." Second, the transplantation metaphor fails to account for transformations that occur in the very process of transferring a legal idea, no matter how hard reformers may try to preserve the initial concept. The organ or plant, it is suggested, is simply cut out in one place and implanted in another. Third, the transplantation metaphor fails to account for the transformations in the receiving system following the transfer of the legal idea. Teubner (1998) has attempted to make up for this last shortcoming of the transplantation metaphor by introducing the allegory of a "legal irritant." While this metaphor is at least capable of capturing the influence exerted by the "irritant" on the receiving system – and possibly also the reverse influence exerted by the receiving system on the irritant – it fails to capture the comparative dimension of legal transfers (Langer 2004: 32). Moreover, this perspective arguably cleaves to a natural scientific, positivistic sort of conceptualization. As White, who warns against an understanding of literary translation according to which the latter is a case of transplantation or, in his terminology, "transportation," puts it:

> [Conceiving of] translation as transportation commits us implicitly to a certain view of meaning, namely that it is like an object that can be picked up out of the place where it is found and dropped into another place; or, to put it another way, that the meaning of a sentence can be separated from its words – from its language, from its cultural context – and reproduced in another (White 1990: 234).

Rehm (2008) is aware of these realities, which is why he tries to bring the various strong and weak versions together to form a workable compromise. This attempt finds its expression in statements such as this: "Beyond the simple adoption of a certain rule in a statute, a successful transplantation has to take into account the institutional structures and conditions, the real application of laws and the teaching of law" (Rehm 2008: 42). Here an obvious difficulty lies in the fact that legal transfer conceived of as transplantation is simply unable to take into account all the factors present in the receiving system Rehm sets out to examine. In his highly insightful elaboration of the various external factors influencing legal transfers, such as nationality, religion, the economy, and the natural environment, Rehm does touch on a number of fundamentally important aspects. In his discussions of the "nation as a socializing unit (*Sozialisationseinheit*)" (Rehm 2008: 20f.), of "law as a function of political conditions" (Rehm 2008, 23), and of "language as a national border" (Rehm 2008: 25 ff.), he succeeds in highlighting the empirical realities and interrelationships of the process he set out to understand and explain. But in doing so, Rehm only scratches the very surface of these aspects. This is probably for the most part due to the fact that it is not his aim to discuss them in any depth, but rather to focus on those factors which have to be taken into account in order to make transplantation successful. That being as it may, Rehm ultimately fails to give sufficient attention to socialization, political struggles, or linguistic factors as potential reasons for making reference to legal ideas and norms from other contexts. Moreover, again due to the epistemological limits of the conception of legal transfer as "transplantation," Rehm misses out on the fact that the aforementioned factors, as well as the various identities they carry with them, are themselves subject to negotiation. In the following, we will see that the translation metaphor, by contrast, does not suffer these major conceptual shortcomings, and that it is able to provide a more analytically comprehensive vocabulary.

2.2 Legal transplantation in practice

Before making the move from transplantation to translation, it is important to analyze the application of the transplantation metaphor to an actual case of legal transfer in a "transitional country" (Song 2000)[5]. This has the advantage of illustrating how the transplantation metaphor not only hampers theorizing, but also practical application. In his legal comparison, Song (2000) analyzes the genesis of Article 8 of the Korean Constitution as a transplantation of the German constitutional provision on political parties to Korea in the early 1960s. What he aims to do is to give a critical analysis of the introduction of Article 8 into the Korean constitution by means of a legal comparison that goes beyond the simple static juxtaposition and mechanical grouping that is all too common to legal research and in essence amounts to little more than a merely descriptive endeavor (Song 2000: 116ff.). In order to overcome these shortcomings by uncovering what he assumes to be the underlying reasons for the poor performance of legal provisions on political parties in Korea, Song adopts a perspective of legal transplantation. He states two reasons for proceeding in this way (Song 2000: 115, FN). First, Song submits, "transplantation" denotes the mere act of taking something out of one place and planting it elsewhere; it provides, he alleges, a purely descriptive analytical device that is value-neutral in and of itself and is capable of capturing all possible acts of reception, those based on agreement as well as those based on coercion. In other words, Song sees a certain "objectivity" in the term insofar as it does not precipitately depict the phenomenon at hand as one of either "imposition" or "reception" only. Second, he maintains, the metaphor of "transplantation" correctly suggests that, just like plants or organs, legal transplants are no mere objects, but are closely associated with the soil or body in which they first came into being, and will come to be equally closely associated with whatever soil or body they find themselves in once they have been transplanted. This, Song holds, can "stimulate the socio-scientific imagination" of the researcher and push him to go beyond

5 In the following, I refer to Song's article as published in the year 2000 in the Seoul National University Law Journal, because it offers more information than its abbreviated translation into English (also contained in this edited volume). In what follows, all translations into English of passages from Song's 2000 article are my translations.

conventional approaches. By opting for a "positive definition of comparative law," Song makes it quite clear, in a similar fashion to Rehm (2008), that the starting point of the inquiry into processes of transfer must be the recognition that the law is not a mere means of organizing and leading society, but is actually closely related to, and associated with, social reality. This brings him to take a socio-legal path that opens onto a critical perspective, one that acknowledges the fact that the law is not simply a given which is merely to be applied, as well as the fact that the enactment and enforcement of individual laws, and their very contents, too, have to be subjected to critical scrutiny. Song then sets out to put this theory into practice by analyzing the factual and legal normative environment of transplantation in Germany and Korea in the early 1960s. Song finally concludes that the genesis of the Korean constitutional provision on political parties was a representative case of "negative assimilation" (Song 2000, 16), in that it did not take into account Korea's "social context," thus relegating the "imported" legal statutes to the status of being merely "decorative." For him, "negative assimilation fails to correspond to the intent of transplantation and is therefore the result of an inherent asynchrony between transplantation and assimilation in the transplantation of statute laws" (Song 2000: 121). A successful transplantation must be undertaken "together with the formation of conditions enabling the transplanted law to perform its function" (Song 2000: 122). However, as Song notes in relation to the Korea of the 1960s, the then authoritarian regime, its secret service, and the "legal notables" appointed in the name of political modernization and progress enacted a law on political parties that was very restrictive in regard to political activities, and thereby stood in contradiction with the constitutional provision on political parties, while at the same time handing major parties a monopoly on elections (Song 2000: 143).

From my point of view, both Song and Rehm (2008) become constrained by terminology such as "transplantation," "assimilation into foreign soil," or "importing country." The former begins his theoretical discussion by stating that "law [...] is not indifferent to social realities," and "legal study means exploring how a legal norm performs its function in a given social context" (Song 2000: 118). Furthermore, in line with Schwarz's contention that "it is just a legal code, not the law that we import" (Schwarz 1960; cited in Song 2000: 121), Song speaks of "social institutions" that are, he submits, indispensable for the proper functioning of transplanted legal statutes. From my standpoint, three aspects of this argumentation reveal the difficulties inherent in trying to explain the complexities of the circulation process by looking through the lens of "transplantation," difficulties which arise from the inherent limitations of that very lens itself. The first problem arises from the fact that once one recognizes, as Song does, that there is a need to both understand and take into account social realities and institutions in trying to understand the functioning of legal norms and institutions, one cannot very well combine that insight with the claim that laws in circulation are foreign "implants." In order to pinpoint this conceptual incompatibility, it is instructive to examine the issue of recipients' bodies rejecting certain transplants or implants. While human recipients' bodies are known to sometimes reject particular transplants or implants on the simple grounds of lacking the required physical constitution for accommodating them, human societies, being discursive concepts and as such open to constant reinterpretation, are far too malleable to ever be considered as categorically lacking a particular "constitution," let alone a physical one. At the same time, the foreign legal ideas and institutions to be incorporated into the receiving societies are themselves nowhere near as clearly and immutably defined as transplants, or implants, into human bodies are. The transplantation metaphor is, accordingly, largely unsuited to capturing the interrelationship and interactivity between a 'receiving' society and 'foreign' legal ideas and institutions. Speaking of "moving a plant from one soil to another," rather than of "organ transplants" or "implants," somewhat widens the field of vision, but nonetheless remains entrenched in the bio-materialistic, not to mention positivistic, frame of the transplantation metaphor, and accordingly fails to capture the wide range of ontological, methodological, and normative aspects of the phenomenon at hand[6]. The second difficulty arises in connection with the fact that those who adhere to the transplantation approach tend to judge the success or failure of what they refer to as an act of transplantation by the criterion of the transplanted norm's supposed "intention." In the case of the introduction of the provision on political parties into the Korean constitution, such intention would evidently refer to that of the initial law as it was made in Germany. However, the transplantation was, in actual fact, carried out by officials in the Korean authoritarian regime and by a number of scholars who were more or less forced to participate in the process (Song 2000: 139f.). So the intention of the transplantation was to indeed restrict parties, while simultaneously giving them sufficient rights to monopolize the institutionalized arena of politics (the national assembly) in order to shore up the regime's power despite the adoption of formally democratic rules. Here it becomes very clear that reversing the initially democratic provision and changing it into an authoritarian one is not an act of simple transplantation, but rather an act of translation. From the translation perspective, at least, the focus would have to be on the "intent" of the translators, not on the intent of the norm. A third problem, as I see it, arises from the fact that while Song provides a lengthy and in-depth discussion of the historical, cultural, and institutional differences

6 See Langer and his critical view of the metaphor of "legal irritants" (Langer 2004: 32).

between the German and the Korean polities, and of the divergences in the respective key actors' strategies and behaviors (Song 2000: 122–129), in the process shedding much light on a number of influential factors, he fails to actually engage with the latter in the further course of his discussion. These factors do not become part of the theoretical arsenal of the transplantation metaphor.

All in all, both Rehm's (2008) and Song's (2000) critical approaches to analyzing the circulation of legal ideas and norms provide rich insight into crucial aspects of this process. Even so, the transplantation metaphor suffers from an evident heuristic shallowness, so much so that, irrespective of how critical and sophisticated a user of that metaphor might be, thinking in terms of "transplantation" will in itself inevitably constrain the quality of their reflection about the circulation of ideas and norms. For this reason, I will now turn to the theoretical potential of the translation metaphor.

2.3 Legal translation in theory

In addition to the notion of legal transplantation (Watson 1974; Freund-Kahn 1974), there is a wide array of other metaphors for analyzing the movement of legal ideas, including: "legal irritant" (Teubner 1998), "legal transformation" (Xu Zhangrun 2004), "legal transposition" (Orücü 2002), "legal reception" (Wieacker 1967), "legal transfer" (Fadé 1993), "legal import" (v. Münch 1994), "convergence/divergence/difference" (Pistor and Wellons 1999), "selective adaptation" (Potter 2004), "institutional monocropping" (Evans 2003), and the like. The pros and cons of these different approaches (and they do offer informative and illuminating insights) have been discussed elsewhere (Perenboom 2012: 45ff.). Here I concentrate mainly on the advantages of the metaphor of "legal translation" (Langer 2004) in contrast to the above-discussed metaphor of legal transplantation, in preparation of the more empirically based chapter below.

The most obvious advantages of the translation metaphor were first put forward by the very scholar who was first to propose it as a heuristic device (Langer 2004: 33–35). These advantages can in turn be fruitfully combined with further suggestions stemming from the policy translation literature (Freeman 2006; Freeman 2009; Johnson and Hagström 2005). The first advantage is that the translation metaphor is inherently analytic in the manner of immanent critique, in opposition to the transplantation metaphor, which is rather descriptive. That point is an important prerequisite for the critical analysis of law and adjudication. Moreover, legal translation is also directly compatible with a wide array of theoretical frameworks. Second, the translation metaphor connotes a comparative perspective in which a distinction is made between a "source" legal system and a "target" legal system. By *source* I do not mean "origin," but a source in the sense of a *point of reference for translation*. Beyond a simple comparison between a "here" and a "there," this metaphor also captures the qualitative dimension of a source language, as well as that of its grammar and the grammar of its receiving counterpart, which puts it at a qualitatively deeper level than that reached through the transplantation metaphor. Accordingly, this makes it possible to account for differences in the source and target language that originate in different structures of interpretation and meaning. By taking this into account, we are made aware of the fact that something can be lost or won along the way in the process of translation. Third, and partly as result of what has already been said, the translation metaphor distinguishes between the original legal idea or institution as developed in the source legal system and the translated idea or institution. Here, then, is an additional differentiation able to account for the change a legal idea undergoes on its "journey," an aspect the transplantation metaphor fails to account for. Again, "original" here does not refer to something supposedly authentic, but to something that serves as the "main point of reference." Fourth, the translation metaphor allows for plurality of authorship, and is thus able to account for yet another potential source of change in ideas in translation.

As with the translation of policies, the translation of legal ideas and norms is partly personal in character – with the translator as the principal actor (Freeman 2009: 433) – and, accordingly, is partly shaped by power relations. In addition to the fact that legal ideas and norms change as such when "traveling," every legislative process involves a plurality of actors with different skills and various backgrounds (Langer 2004: 35), to say nothing of the distinct institutional power relations these actors find themselves in (Johnson and Hagström 2005: 372) or the institutional positions they occupy (Schmidt 2008). Moreover, as people come and go, and ideas and positions change, the balance of power changes, too, and institutionalized ideas come to be challenged accordingly. Fifth, translation is understood to be always anchored in local contexts, to be an activity that primarily takes place at the "receiving end" (Johnson and Hagström 2005: 370–372). This is because translation always serves a purpose, and therefore an interest, which taken together means that a legal idea is never merely carried over, or passively received from the divine, but that it actively takes over, or reinvents, its original (Freeman 2009: 434). Only with an authoritative translation can a new idea be taken over and successfully – that is, convincingly (Schmidt 2008: 313ff.) – be translated.

To summarize the advantages of the translation metaphor, it can be said that it provides the researcher, the legislator, and the legal practitioner with a bundle of epistemologically sensitizing conceptualizations of reality, including political processes of policy and law making. So, to say that a legal idea or norm is translated implies understanding and analyzing the phenomenon in the framework of post-positivist theory and method. The metaphor makes it possible for all actors, including scholars and practitioners, to see down to the bottom of the pond they are swimming in.

3. From metaphor to method

How do we derive actual methodological instruments for empirical research from these theoretical heights from which we are said to see so much more clearly? This is the issue to which I shall now turn. It is first necessary to take a step back and look at a number of theoretical considerations advanced by various constructivist strands before we can make the leap forward toward an empirically workable framework of analysis. First of all, by using the heuristic device of translation, it is possible to perform an epistemological turn to interpretivism (see Freeman 2006: 12). This operation increases analytical reach by stretching further in vertical, horizontal, and diagonal terms, in other words, in terms of height, width, and depth (Freeman 2006: 2). It generates the potential to capture the dynamics, the contingency, and the open-endedness[7] of the continuously evolving process that is the travel of ideas.

3.1 Theoretical considerations: constructive discourses, discursive constructions

How then can we exploit this theoretical potential for practice? Being able to do so is crucially important if we want to analyze (which requires more than just "breaking something down into its constituent parts") the kinds of legal ideas and norms that are translated between countries, and how and why they are being so translated. We have to be able to explain how the different parts come together, how they are being constructed, deconstructed, and reconstructed. The ideas in and of themselves – in spite of finding themselves at the heart of the analysis on the grounds of being the very objects of the transfer process under examination – cannot provide sufficient information on why it is that they move, and how they do so. Rather, ideas have to be understood in their interaction with the discourse

---

7 This aspect is also stressed by Johnson and Hagström (2005), who point out disembedding, objectifying, traveling, institutionalizing, de-institutionalizing, and re-institutionalizing processes in the overall process of translation (Johnson and Hagström 2005: 372).

by which they are being conveyed – and which they carry at the same time. Only by using the concept of discourse can "we simultaneously indicate the ideas represented in the discourse [...] and the interactive processes by which ideas are conveyed" (Schmidt 2008: 309).[8] Similar to public policy (Freeman 2006: 4), legal norms can be said to be social constructs, and adjudication, too, is a highly discursive endeavor (Lee 2007: 10ff.; Müller 1989), not to mention the fact that "the activity of translation" can be said to stand "[a]t the center of law" (White 1990: 246). In this discursive process, "phenomena that did not seem to be connected to each other become organized in a consistent argumentative structure," such that "one set of relationships or associations [comes to be substituted] with another" (Freeman 2006: 5). Drawing on Schmidt's *discursive institutionalism* (DI), we can assume two realms of discourse activity. In the realm of "coordinative discourse," high-level policy actors, including members of government, members of political parties, members of parliamentary committees, and various other policy experts, interact with a view to creating legal norms. The realm of "communicative discourse," by contrast, comprises the interaction between these high-level policy actors and the general public, the mass media, and/or civil society organizations (Schmidt 2008: 308). Agency comes into play through social learning or teaching in the form of spiral storytelling, which involves the unfolding of storylines (Hajer 1995: 56; 62f.; Hajer 2008: 216 ff.)[9] in sequential episodes that propel a certain discursive frame (similarly Freeman 2009: 434). In the process, consolidated ideas and norms are challenged, structured, institutionalized, and finally re-consolidated (see Mosler 2012: 28), to exist in this re-consolidated form until such time when they will no longer appear to capture the problems of the day and when their application will no longer yield satisfactory results. This will lead to a new generation of ideas legitimizing new statutes, and their enforcement, by providing structures and patterns that are able to make sense of new phenomena (see Schmidt 2002: 309; also Freeman 2006: 2).

---

8 The Sino-Korean term for discourse is *tamnon,* which consists of the characters 談 (tam) and 論 (non). While the latter can be translated as "discuss, talk, argue, comment, treat, or deal with," the former character is usually translated as "a talk, a story, or a tale." Remarkable is the fact that the character 談 consists of two different subcharacters, with 言 meaning "to speak or talk" and 火 denoting "(camp) fire." This fact seems of interest in relation to Freeman's conception of "public policy assuming some of the functions of the camp fire" (Freeman 2006: 2), which, of course, refers back to Lyotard (1990) and his idea of "modern storytellers."

9 The essential role of storylines is threefold, comprising knowledge clustering, the positioning of actors, and the creation of discourse coalitions (Hajer 1997: 63).

So, if we follow Freeman in arguing that the "authority [of an idea or norm] comes not from originality, but from authoritative translation" (Freeman 2006: 4; my addition), then we might ask: what makes the translation of a norm "authoritative"? The success of a discourse that favors certain legal ideas or norms depends upon whether it is able to generate a coherent picture of, or frame for, the norm (be it a statutory law in its entirety or an individual legal provision) to be realized within the relevant wider body of law (such as all the laws related to the political process or to political parties) and within the given social context of a particular polity as shaped, among other things, by current public opinion (see Schmidt 2002: 309; similar Hajer 1997: 59).

In other words, the more normatively convincing and cognitively justified the idea behind the norm being conveyed, the higher the likelihood that it will be successfully realized.[10] Part of this *argumentative approach* (Hajer 1995; 1997) emphasizes the importance of the institutional power position of the various actors to the manner in which the discourse competition unfolds (Hajer 1997: 63; Johnson and Hagström 2005: 372; Schmidt 2010: 18ff.).[11] For a discourse to become hegemonic and its constituent ideas to become reality in the form of actual legal norms or adjudication – that is, for a translation to become authoritative – that discourse has to win the respective continuously evolving discourse competition. This competition takes place between various *discourse coalitions* (Hajer 1997: 58ff.), each feeding on its respective actors' involvement in the form of storytelling, and generates narratives that solidify into certain frames. Discourse coalitions are not only defined by their actors, but also by the storylines set forth by these actors, and by the practices in which discursive activity is embedded, or, to be more accurate, by all these factors taken together (Hajer 1997: 65). Based on these theoretical considerations, how should we proceed in our empirical analysis?

3.2 The analytical approach: tracking down translation

The analytical approach is based on asking questions about the different (con-)texts of the translation process. Answering these analytical questions

10 While the (cognitive) necessity of the norm has to be proven on the strength of its relevance, applicability, coherence, and capacity, its (normative) appropriateness has to be conveyed by showing how it solves the problem at hand, while simultaneously harmonizing with prevailing currents of public opinion (Schmidt 2002: 309).

11 Thus, the potential discursive power of an actor does not solely depend on his objective position of power, but equally on his subjective, i.e. individually perceived, position of power (Schmidt 2010: 18). This way of thinking is similar to that involved in the "balance of threat" theory (Walt 1985).

makes it possible to scrutinize the empirical data effectively with the aim of tracking down the dynamics and mechanisms of the translation process. The questions point to the three main dimensions, or texts, of discursive intercourse: institutional contexts (power structures, power positions, and actors); actors' texts (in other words, their storylines); and the final discursive artifacts (actual manifestations of the discourse).

The first question is: who is talking? To ask who is talking is to identify an actor's formal and de facto position of institutional power. By "formal power" I mean the power officially vested in the actor in keeping with his role in the system, such as, for example, the legislative power vested in an assemblyman in contrast to, say, a professor or any other member of the general public. By "de facto power" I mean the authority an actor can achieve and wield depending on how he is perceived by others. For example, the de facto power of a president typically fades toward the end of his term even though nothing changes institutionally through the mere passage of time. Korea has known a wide variety of political systems, ranging from fully-fledged dictatorship to consolidating democracy, which is why, in my analysis of who is talking, I will differentiate along the lines of the specific supra-contexts of (a) monopolized; (b) oligopolized; and (c) multitudinal translations in authoritative regimes, regimes in transition to democracy, and formally democratic regimes respectively.

The second question to ask is: what is being said? The following six questions aim at reconstructing the lines of reasoning typically advanced by the various actors engaged in what might be called processes of *argumentative rationalization* (Hajer 1995):[12] (1) What is perceived to be the problem, how is it defined and presented? (2) What is perceived to be the origin of the problem?; (3) What is said to be the likely outcome of continued inaction? (4) What is proposed by way of a solution to the problem?; (5) What are said to be the specific benefits of the proposed solution?; and (6) What are the principles, values, norms, and concepts drawn upon in trying to legitimize the proposed solution? (cf. Viehöver 2006: 197ff.; Viehöver 2004: 253ff.)

With these analytical tools I shall scrutinize the provision on political parties in the Korean Constitution (hereafter: KC) and the Korean Political Parties

12 Here I am loosely following the models of reconstructive investigation put forward by Viehöver and by Johnson and Hagström (Viehöver 2006: 197; Johnson and Hagström 2005: 374). This method is also in keeping with the theoretical assumptions of Freeman (2006), who states that policies, by virtue of their narrative structure and their quality as collective scripts, define a collective problem, a solution, and a course of action (Freeman 2006: 2).

Act (hereafter: PPA), which together stand at the very center of Korean law and adjudication regarding political parties. The first legal norms for political parties in Korea can be traced back to minor preliminary statutes formed right after liberation from Japanese colonial rule under the United States Army Military Government in Korea (hereafter: USAMGIK) in the 1940s. These norms were then followed by the introduction of a constitutional clause in 1960 and the enactment of the PPA in 1962. The constitutional clause as well as the PPA were reformed many times over and have continuously evolved from the time of the authoritarian regimes right up until today's formally democratic regimes.

In order to make the analysis feasible, I will narrow my field of inquiry to *party organization on the ground*. First, party organization is a particularly prominent aspect of both Korea's constitutional provision on political parties and of its "prescriptive" (Janda 2005) PPA. Second, the organization and regulation of parties are central aspects of the definition of political parties more generally. Parties are by definition collective organizations whose key function is to put into practice (or *translate*) their representation of the (political will of the) people, and to recruit and select political personnel. Third, party organization, and its transformation, finds itself at the very heart of recent, global trends in party evolution (e.g. the emergence of the cartel party), which makes it a very meaningful subject for comparison.

4. South Korean translations of legal norms concerning political parties

Laws on political parties were first introduced in Korea in the 1940s and 50s, and continue to be amended, in patchwork fashion, on a regular basis even today. In order to capture the full picture of legal translation in its various dimensions at one and the same time, I will use a method of triangulation by examining horizontal, diagonal, and vertical translations respectively, in other words, by conducting a cross-country comparison, a time series analysis, and, finally, a review of adjudication (see Freeman 2006: 3). The cross-country comparison comprises the period between 1945 and 1962, and focuses essentially on reforms made after the military coup in the early 1960s. The subsequent time series analysis spans the period from the end of the 1960s to the present. Finally, the review of exemplary adjudication examines two constitutional decisions made in the early 2000s. For each major revision of norms, the newly resulting legal text, together with the official reasoning advanced to back up the reform in question, is taken as an empirical signifier, or manifestation, of the act of translation. German legal norms on political parties will serve as a benchmark for relative comparison. Narrative structures will be analyzed by identifying storylines and their constituent episodes. This will make it possible to verify specific discourse trends that influence processes of translation, authorizing certain ideas and institutions, and foreclosing others (see Freeman 2009: 434).[13]

4.1 The horizontal dimension: legal translations made from scratch

A. Preliminary traces of legal norms

The very first legal provisions on political parties in Korea can be found as early as 1945, only two months after liberation (i.e., after the unconditional surrender of the Imperial Japanese Army on August 15, 1945), in the form of USAMGIK Ordinance No. 16 on "Affixing Name Signs of Political Parties and Companies." This ordinance mentioned political parties but did not regulate them in any significant way. Only in early 1946, with USAMGIK Ordinance No. 55 titled the "Regulation of Political Parties," did the first noteworthy legal provisions regarding political parties come into existence. These were geared toward a rigid regulation of the activities of political parties. The latter were under an obligation to register with the USAMGIK if they had more than three members, the aim being to compel all kinds of collective political activity to come to the surface as a way of controlling the political landscape. The next legal regulation of political parties followed in 1952 and can be understood as a counter-measure to the restrictive implementation of the ordinance, and to the repeated fraud and malpractice of the governing party. With the "Act on Political Movements," the majority of the Second National Assembly intended to prevent further intervention by the government during election campaigning and to secure the freedom of the activities of political parties (Office of the National Assembly 1992: 9064; cited in Song 2000: 127). However, even though the law was passed in the parliament's plenary session, the Rhee government (Rhee Syngman or Yi Sŭng-man; 1948~1960) did not approve it and even submitted a bill for the abolishment of the law a year later, only to resort to the very statute it had meant to abolish in 1959 when looking for legal grounds to dissolve the Progressive Party (Song 2000: 127), which was perceived to be threatening the regime, especially due to

---

13 It is obvious that official reasoning always accounts for only half of the story. Nonetheless, it remains a part of the overall plot I am attempting to decode. The layer of official reasoning is the very layer of the translation process that must be looked into in order to find out what kinds of contents are reflected in a law resulting from translation, or, to put it differently, what kinds of contents are manifested in the artefact that is the translated law. Official reasoning may not necessarily speak the truth, but nonetheless lays bare the result of the translation.

its increasingly popular leader, Cho Bong-Am. A year after that, the "Registration of Newspapers and Political Parties Act" was passed (July 1, 1960). The law stipulated that parties must report their names, platforms, policy programs, and legal statutes immediately upon their establishment, and must register with the authorities. In addition, it demanded that parties report regularly on their membership numbers, their political activities, and their finances. The KC mentioned political parties as early as in 1948, yet did so only in the general statements contained in its preamble and without assigning political parties any specific rights or duties. It was not until the constitutional review following the April Revolution of 1960, and after former President Rhee Syngman stepped down and went into exile, that Article 13 was created in the second chapter of the KC ("Citizens' Rights and Duties"), which, among other things, stated that "[p]olitical parties enjoy the protection of the State" and that political parties "can be dissolved in accordance with the decision of the Constitutional Court." (see table A-1)[14]

In May 1961, less than one year after Rhee's authoritarian regime had been overthrown and the opposition camp under Prime Minister Chang Myun (Chang Myŏn) had taken power, General Park Chung-Hee (Pak Chŏng-hŭi; 1961–1979) led a military coup, overthrowing the still young government and establishing a rigid military dictatorship. The junta installed the Revolutionary Military Committee which, among others things, reformed a number of important laws and newly enacted a number of equally important laws. In the wake of the military coup of May 1961, all regulations on political parties were suspended, all parties dissolved (by the "Sixth Proclamation of the Revolutionary Military Committee"), and statutes on political parties provisionally replaced by the "Purification Law on Political Activities." General Park was essentially the author of this statute. His was the loudest voice and, with his seizure of power, it became the only one in town. The story he told in order to justify his coup mainly involved framing existing politics and politicians as "inefficient," "anachronistic," and "incapable," all of which, he claimed, led to "unproductive" politics. According to this story, these problems could only be solved through a Korean-style democracy, since Korea had a "unique constitution." As we shall see, this narrative of efficiency and

14 Previously, the authority to dissolve political parties had rested solely with the administration (see below), which means that the addition of this last provision can be seen as great progress in terms of the rights of political parties (see Pak Il-Kyŏng 1986; cited in Song 2000, 128). Furthermore, the Constitutional Court Act enacted on April 15th 1961 complemented the new constitutional provision on political parties by its articles 12, 13, and 22, which regulated the Court's exclusive right to dissolve political parties (Song 2000: 128).

Koreanness runs like a common thread through all translations of legal ideas and norms on political parties around the time of the military coup of 1961.

The authoritarian regime followed a threefold strategy in building their party and executing related reforms of the law. The first part of the strategy was to establish the Democratic Republican Party (DRP). As part of a grand plan to maintain its power over the long term, the regime not only set up this hegemonic party, but also officially forbade all political activity. In order to install a fully-fledged "hegemonic party" (Kim 1989; 1992) with a huge membership base, Kim Jong-Pil (Kim Chong-p'il), founder and head of the new Korean Central Intelligence Agency (KCIA; established in June 1961) and mastermind of the founding of the DRP, made full use of all financial and informational resources of the KCIA and the state apparatus as a whole. Civil servants who were at his disposal facilitated the setting up of party branches, down to the smallest units at the lowest administrational levels. The DRP was equipped with a power structure that was designed to appear democratic on the outside, while, in fact, securing absolute control both inside and outside the party.

The second part of the strategy was to add Article 7 (on political parties) to the constitution, which resembled Article 21 of the German Constitution (Song 2000: 134) and which seems to have been far ahead of the social, cultural, and political realities of the time (see table A-1). The provision guarantees the freedom, plurality, protection, and funding of parties; it demands internal party democracy and whatever organizational arrangements are required to participate in the formation of the political will of the people; it also provides that parties can be dissolved by the constitutional court. Remarkably, Article 7 (today Article 8) was moved to the first chapter of the KC, which marks a deviation from both the previous Korean constitution and the provision Article 7 is modeled on, the German constitutional provision on political parties (see table 4–1 below). In another notable contrast to the German model, the KC explicitly states that "Political parties must have the necessary organizational arrangements to participate in the formation of the political will of the people."[15]

15 It is interesting to note that many of the English versions of the Korean Constitution mistranslate this sentence. The correct, that is, literal, translation of the provision reads "Parties […] shall have the necessary organizational arrangements to participate in the formation of the political will of the people." However, the translations provided by the Constitutional Court (http://korea.assembly.go.kr/res/low_01_read.jsp [accessed 27 March 2012]), by the National Assembly (http://www.ccourt.go.kr/home/att_file/download/Constitution_of_the_Republic_of_Korea.pdf [accessed 27 March 2012]), and even by international organizations such as the UNHCR (http://www.unhcr.org/

Table 2: Comparison of provisions concerning political parties in the current Korean constitution and the Basic Law (German constitution)[16]

	Korean Constitution		**Basic Law**
	I. General Provisions		II. The Federation and the Länder
	Article 8		Article 21
1	...may be freely established.	1	...may be freely established.
	A plural party system is guaranteed.		*[no express provision, but implied]*
2	...must be democratic in their objectives, organization, and activities.		...internal organization must conform to democratic principles.
	...must have the necessary organizational arrangements to participate in the formation of the political will of the people.		...shall participate in the formation of the political will of the people. *[no express provision in the Basic Law, but implied; related provision in the German Political Parties Act (PartG)]*
3	...enjoy the protection of the State.		*[no express provision, but implied]*
	...may be provided with operational funds by the State under the conditions as prescribed by law.		*[no express provision, but implied]*
	[no express provision, but implied in the PPA]		...must publicly account for their assets and for the sources and use of their funds.
4	If the purposes or activities of a political party are contrary to the fundamental democratic order, the Government may bring action against it in the Constitutional Court for its dissolution.	2	Parties that, by reason of their aims or the behavior of their adherents, seek to undermine or abolish the free democratic basic order or to endanger the existence of the Federal Republic of Germany shall be unconstitutional.
	Political parties are dissolved in accordance with the decision of the Constitutional Court.		The Federal Constitutional Court shall rule on the question of unconstitutionality.
	[no express provision, but implied]	3	Details shall be regulated by federal laws.

The Basic Law makes no express provision for this aspect, but a related provision can be found in Article 7, Paragraph 1, Sentence 3 of the German Political Parties Act.[17] The major changes in comparison to Article 13 of the preceding

refworld/docid/3ae6b4dd14.html [accessed 27 March 2012]) all read "Parties [...] shall have the necessary organizational arrangements for the people to participate in the formation of the political will" (my emphasis).

16 Excerpts only. Korean constitutional provisions: my translation; Basic Law: http://www.gesetze-im-internet.de/.

17 Article 7, Paragraph 1, Sentence 3 of the German Political Parties Act provides that "[t]he division into regions must be developed to an extent that will allow individual

Constitution lie in the introduction of the freedom to establish parties and of the obligation both to be democratic in terms of internal structure and to have the necessary organizational arrangements to fulfill the constitutional duty of participating in the formation of the political will of the people. Also, in a clear shift toward an excessively strong party state (Kwŏn 1998: 95), provisions were added requiring that candidates standing in general (Article 36, Paragraph 3) or in presidential elections (Article 64, Paragraph 3) be nominated by the party of which they are a member, and introducing the rule that members of the national assembly will lose their status as parliamentarians should they choose to change their party affiliation (Article 38). Another alteration concerned the substitution of the Constitutional Court as the constitutional organ in charge of the dissolution of political parties with the Supreme Court. However, as we shall see when discussing the enactment of the Political Parties Act, this alteration actually had the effect of restricting the freedom of parties, and the requirement of a well-developed division into regions was abused to effect better control over, and facilitate the mobilization of, the populace in general, and the electorate in particular. Compared to the constitution of 1960, the amendments made after 1961 appear to represent great progress; however, a closer look at their German role model and their actual practical application reveals that the legal ideas imported from Germany had, in fact, been turned on their heads.

The third part of the strategy involved laying a foundation for the formal institutionalization of a pluralistic party system with the enactment of the Political Parties Act in December 1962. The PPA was of a "prescriptive type" (Janda 2005) in that it set (overly) high minimum standards for the overall number of founding members, the number of party chapters, and the number of party-chapter members required to establish a political party, to name only a few of the PPA's stipulations regarding party organization (see table A-2). To this day, the first sentence of the PPA states that it "has the objective of contributing to the sound development of democratic politics by guaranteeing that political parties have the necessary organizational arrangements in order to participate in the formation of the political

---

members to appropriately participate in the formation of the will of the party" (my translation). Of course, there is a difference between "form[ing] the political will of the people" in the Korean provision and "form[ing] the will of the party" in the German provision. More important, however, is the fact that both provisions expressly stipulate organizational structures that will allow for proper individual participation. That being said, the requirement would seem to be stronger in nature in the case of Korea, on the grounds of being included in the constitution. We will come back to this particularity below.

will of the people, and that the organization and the activities of political parties be democratic" (PPA, Article 1; my translation)[18]. In addition, it details the "necessary organizational arrangements" by stating that a party has to have party chapters in more than one third of the overall number of electoral districts, that it has to have more than 50 members in each of its party chapters, and that it has to distribute the minimum number of party chapters over at least five cities or provinces (of which two must be Seoul and Busan, while the remaining three or more cities or provinces can be freely determined) (PPA 1962, Art. 25–27). The official reason given for the enactment of the PPA was to "guarantee a sound pluralist party system[,] to prevent the emergence of too high a number of small parties, [and] to live up to the demands of the constitution" (PPA 1962 Bill). After all, the reasoning continues, the revision of the constitution had been undertaken to "demand the democratic organization and activities of political parties [and] regulate the scope of political parties [...] in order to realize a sound political party system" (PPA 1962 Bill).

Table 3: Constitutional provisions on political parties and other legal provisions concerning political parties (1945–1963)

Date of enactment / Date of enforcement	Name of statute or other legal provision
October 24th, 1945 / November 3rd, 1945	"Affixing Name Signs of Political Parties and Companies" (USAMGIK Ordinance No. 16)
February 23rd, 1946 / February 24rd, 1946	"Regulation of Political Parties" (USAMGIK Ordinance No. 55)
July 17th, 1948 / July 17th, 1948	Preamble to the KC
April 16th, 1952 (approval)	"Act on Political Movements"
June 15th, 1960 / June 15th, 1960	Article 13 of the KC, provision on political parties
July 30th, 1960 / July 30th, 1960	"Registration of Newspapers and Political Parties Act"
May 22nd, 1961 / May 22nd, 1961	"Sixth Proclamation by the Revolutionary Military Committee"
March 16th, 1962 / March 16th, 1962	"Purification Law on Political Activities" (abolished Dec. 19th, 2008)
December 12th, 1962 / January 1st, 1963	"Political Parties Act"
December 26th, 1962/ December 17th, 1963	Article 7 of the KC, provision on political parties

18 In what follows, all translations from Korean into English of passages from the PPA are my translations.

In sum, the institution of the political party was designed to form a part of the authoritarian regime's system of control that was, among other things, geared towards making the junta appear to be ruling "by legal means" in spite of the illegality of its seizure of power and the resulting overall illegitimacy of its rule. In order to formally legalize what was essentially illegitimate, the regime not only amended the constitution, but also enacted a separate Political Parties Act and established a seeming paragon of a political party in the form of the DRP. The result was the institutionalization of an officially and formally democratic, but unofficially and informally corrupt, authoritarian regime. A prominent commentator of the time characterized these translations as "the pursuit of modernity at the expense of politics, while in the process failing to achieve the one because of their neglect of the other" (Huntington 1968: 92).

4.2 The diagonal dimension – translational evolution over time

Whereas the above elaborations focused on the immediate changes that occurred right after the military's seizure of power and its attempt to install a rigid political system, I shall now concentrate on the dynamic changes that have transpired between then and now. The relevant period of time stretches from the late 1960s to the present day and can be divided into three sub-periods: the authoritarian regimes (1969~1986), formal democratization (1987~1997), and neoliberalization (1998~2010). The main question is: How were the legal ideas related to, and the norms on, political parties translated during the military dictatorships, after democratization, and after neoliberalization respectively? What has changed, what has stayed the same, and why?

A. The period of authoritarian rule (1969~1986)

The Park regime (1961~1979) was obviously characterized by the dictator and his aides holding a monopoly on translation. From setting up the Revolutionary Military Committee following the coup in the spring of 1961 to introducing the Yushin system in October 1972, Park was in control of the various "state apparatuses" (Althusser 1976) and remained so until his death. These apparatuses translated all information in a way that accorded with the great leader's ideas. The translation of "democracy" was especially unambiguous and explicitly "Korean" for the entire duration of Park's reign (Kang 2011). Research has shown that Park rejected "Western democracy," more specifically its "direct importation from the West" (Park 1962: 230) or "transplantation" into Korea (Park 1979: 46), because it did not, he claimed, "fit the Korean history and cultural traditions" (Park 1974: 307) or the "Korean (physical) constitution" (Park 1963: 254). His strong belief was that the experiment with Western democracy had failed, and he consequently endorsed a "Korean-style democracy." During the period of the military junta (1961~1963), Park advocated what he called an "administrative democracy," only to speak of a "national democracy" during his time as the fifth and sixth president (1963~1972), and, finally, of a "Korean-style democracy" in the period of time following the Yushin reforms (1972~1979).[19] He made a bogeyman both of the Rhee regime, which he referred to as "corrupt," and of the brief period of Democratic Party rule that followed it, which he liked to characterize as "chaotic." These, he claimed, were the kinds of "experiments with political democracy" that led to nothing but rivalry between factions, chaos, waste, and inefficiency. He, on the other hand, Park maintained, was in pursuit of a type of democracy and a style of politics that was "efficient" or "productive" (Kang 2011: 312). The New Village Movement (*saemaŭlundong*) he instigated can be seen as an example of politics in the name of efficiency and productivity. In essence, this movement organized the rural populace into local networks and mobilized these networks via propaganda projects specifically geared toward the countryside, all this in the name of making rural Koreans "participate efficiently" in government policies (Kang 2011: 315). Against this background, the translations of legal provisions related to political parties can be deemed to have been quite convincing in the way they fitted in with the overall construction of the modern Korea of the 1960s and 1970s.

The PPA's revision in 1969 saw alterations that bolstered an already very prescriptive statute. The minimum overall number of party chapters was raised from one third to half of the total number of electoral districts for the general election, and the minimum total number of members for each party chapter was raised from fifty to one hundred. Officially, this was "to prevent the emergence of too high a number of small parties and to promote the establishment of a sound two-party system" (PPA Bill 1969).[20] The constitutional reform of 1972 produced only minor changes for the provision on political parties. The only addition was

19 On October 27, 1972, the daily newspaper Donga Ilbo quotes Park as saying that "we should not use up any more of our precious national energy for imitating foreign democracies, we have to indigenize them." This statement marks the official beginning of the story of Park's "Korean-style democracy."

20 That requirements concerning party membership and party organization were thus made stricter is hardly surprising in light of the fact that the regime had come under increasing pressure from protesters and was faced with both the threat of poor results in the presidential and parliamentary elections of 1967 and increasingly tense relations with North Korea.

to deem unconstitutional any attempts at "endangering the state",[21] while the only other change was to substitute the Supreme Court by a Constitutional Committee. This last change stands out for marking the turn from authoritative regime to blunt dictatorship. Not least by thereby translating the Supreme Court into a Constitutional Committee that was easier for him to manipulate, President Park acquired almost absolute control of state power.

At first glance, the revision of the PPA of 1972 would seem to contradict these findings, given that the regulation of political parties was, in fact, softened (see table A-2). This, however, needs to be qualified in light of the fact that Park was bestowed with the right to appoint one third of the overall number of assembly members (KC 1972, Article 40).[22] In other words, there was no longer any need to be so restrictive with political parties, which led Park to use this "softening" reform as a strategic counterweight to his radical reforms. This is also evident from the official reasoning to the PPA, according to which the PPA was designed "to guarantee the greatest possible freedom for party establishment [...] and to delete unnecessary regulations in light of the revised constitution" (PPA Bill 1972).

Following the assassination of President Park by the chief of his very own secret service at the end of 1979, another military officer, Chun Doo-Hwan (Chŏn Tu-hwan), took power in early 1980 and subsequently remodeled the constitution, albeit only moderately so. Translations remained as monopolized as before, and the story of "Korean democracy" stayed almost the same, even if it was now told in a slightly different tone. Chun had to distance himself from the harsh dictatorial rule of his predecessor, and in so doing even went so far as to add to the provision on political parties the right of parties to receive state funds (see table A-1). However, this was not only part of his strategy to appear modern and democratic, but also part of his plans for controlling the party system by novel means. Contrary to the strategy of the Park regime, which in the end no longer

---

21 While this phrase had existed in the German Basic Law ("den Bestand der Bundesrepublik Deutschland zu gefährden"), it had not been translated in Korea. However, the phrase was erased as part of the constitutional reform in 1980 (see table A-1).

22 In addition, the minimum number of party chapters was reduced to one third, instead of one half, of the total number of electoral districts. Also, the number of electoral districts was reduced to 73 as a result of converting what formerly were "single-member districts" into "multi-member districts." Moreover, the minimum number of party members in individual party chapters was also reduced, dropping from 100 to 50. As a result, the overall minimum number of party chapter members was reduced to about 1200.

tried to hide the fact that it exercised control by an arbitrary majority, the Chun regime opted for a strategy of divide and rule. Politicians from the potential opposition were once again allowed to become active in political parties, but only so long as they behaved well. The strategy was to divide political forces into many different *satellite parties*, to make them financially dependent on the regime's good will, and thus to *play at* democracy. This is also reflected in revisions of the PPA lowering the bar with regard to the minimum number of founders and the minimum number of party chapters required to establish a political party, as well as with regard to the requirements for becoming a party member (see table A-2). According to the official reasoning for these reforms, they were aimed at fostering the "formation of the political will of the people" by ensuring that political parties were organized in a manner facilitating their establishment and subsistence, and by ensuring that the composition of the government reflected the political, economic, social, and cultural diversity of the country and its people. The latter was supposed to be achieved "by greatly opening the door for participation in political parties" (PPA Bill 1980).

B. *After formal democratization (1987~1997)*

Things really took a turn with the democratization process setting in at the end of the 1980s. The democratization movement of the 1980s grew steadily stronger and came to a climax in the summer of 1987, forcing the military regime to give in and prepare a revised version of the constitution that was subsequently democratically approved by the majority of the people. This is the constitution that is still in force today. The arena of institutionalized politics was thrown wide open. Translations shifted from being monopolized to being oligopolized.[23] In constitutional terms, the great political transformations of the time were reflected in the setting up of a Constitutional Court largely modeled on its German counterpart (Ginsburg 2010: 3).[24] The constitutional provision on political parties,

23 It is a well-known fact that a total number of eight representatives from both the regime party and the main opposition party negotiated the compromise version of the new constitution in 1987. On the one hand, this compromise was seen as a huge progress in the sense that, for the first time, the constitution was reformed on the basis of actual negotiations between major players in Korean politics; on the other, it was criticized for the elitist (oligarchic) nature of the process of its formation on the grounds that the interests of other interest groups, such as those representing workers, were not accounted for.

24 There are several aspects of this particular revision that have been labeled insufficient. They are said to be a result of the fact that even though many of those involved in the

however, was barely altered (see table A-1), mostly because it already met formal democratic standards in its then shape. The PPA, by contrast, did undergo revision in 1989. Reflecting the then prevailing general trend toward formal democratization, the necessary minimum number of party chapters was reduced from one fourth to one fifth of the total number of electoral districts for the general election, thus reducing the minimum number of party members required for party registration by 50% (see table A-3). The official reason for doing so was wanting to "secure the establishment and the activities of democratic parties and to extend the opportunities of the people to participate in politics." In the same vein, the new PPA was said to be an attempt to "widen the range of freedoms for party activities in order to invigorate party politics [...]" (PPA Bill 1989).[25] Also, the new constitution raised the number of electoral districts to more than 200 in order to optimize the representation of the populace by its parliamentary representatives.[26] The revision of the PPA a few years later in 1993 under the first civilian president to follow decades of military dictatorship, Kim Young-Sam (Kim Yŏng-sam; 1993~1998), saw an additional softening of restrictions. The minimum number of party chapters was reduced to one tenth of the overall number of electoral districts (see Appendix, table A-2). Again, this reform was intended to "extend the opportunities of the people to participate in politics and to institutionally secure the ability of political parties to operate autonomously and thereby build more solid roots with the people" (PPA Bill 1993).

C. *After Neoliberalization (1998~2010)*[27]

Yet another turn occurred at the end of the 1990s. The financial crisis setting in at the end of 1997, together with the subsequent provision of a loan facility by the International Monetary Fund and its attendant economic restrictions, had a major impact on almost every aspect of society. As a result, general public opinion became even more predisposed to ideas and narratives of "efficiency" and "small government." The crisis, which was both immediate and material in

---

negotiations for reform were from the so-called democracy movement, the relevant discussions were ultimately conducted behind closed doors between a mere handful of politicians.

25 In practical terms, this meant that it had become possible for parties to install party branches at the administrational levels of the *ŭp* (towns), the *myŏn* (townships), and the tong (boroughs).

26 The reform of the Public Election Act (PEA) saw the reintroduction of single-member districts with a view to "realizing the development of democratic politics" (PEA Bill).

27 This section draws partly on Mosler (2012) and Mosler (2013).

nature, served as a key event in exposing the discrepancies between the expectations and the realities of Korean state affairs. In working toward first defining and then overcoming this crisis, the new government under Kim Dae-Jung (Kim Tae-jung; 1998–2003) came to comply with, and propagate, a *discourse of efficiency*. This was partly a result of "discourse affinity" (Hajer 2003) between the neoliberal narrative of reconstruction and the anti-corruption storyline that presented the crisis as a product of the preceding government's failure to address the corrupt relationship between politics and business (see Kang 2005: 284f.). Due to this affinity, the neoliberal narrative of reconstruction and the anti-corruption storyline ultimately came to display a common discursive ground of neoliberal efficiency. The Kim Dae-Jung government tried to solve the problem of state entanglement with business by subjecting the country's major business conglomerates to strict neoliberal market discipline (Kim and Song, 2000). Put differently, the logic of efficient and lean business practice was used as an antidote to corruption. This, of course, flung the door wide open for a neoliberal way of thinking. Up until this point in time, the main focus of general interest had not been on politics, but on economic questions. Politics became a focus only after the full extent of the failures in economic policy, and of the collusion between the state and the *chaebol*, had come to light. While deliberations on political reforms in the media, among scholars, and in the general population had visibly been set in motion with the onset of the crisis, it took several more years for the efficiency discourse to begin to manifest itself.

Once it did, the arena of translation was thrown open even wider, enabling a multitude of translators to participate. Activities on the part of NGOs and other organizations were not only welcomed, but actively encouraged and supported. Civil society was allowed to have a stronger say than in the past. In 1999, members of the parliamentary sub-committee on the reform of political party law held substantial debates on what to do about the institution of party chapters.[28] In doing so, they portrayed party chapters as being at the heart of "old-style" Korean politics, which they characterized as "inefficient and costly." While the amendment of the Political Parties Act in February 2000 did not involve any changes to political party organization as such, it did limit the employment of salaried personnel to central party branches, city party branches and provincial party branches, thereby implicitly precluding the employment of paid staff at

28 Party chapters constitute the party on the ground in the respective electoral districts. Given that they had often been found to be the scene of corruption and malpractice, demands for their abolition had been made since the early 1990s.

the level of party chapters or below (PPA 2000). For the first time, the narrative of tackling "high-cost, low-efficiency politics (by limiting the number of paid staff)" found its way into the text of a law proposal (namely into the PPA Bill 2000), reflecting the fact that the discursive field of political party reform had been structured around a fresh focus on efficiency. This is also in keeping with an amendment of the Election Law of the time that cut down the number of parliamentary seats from 299 to 273 (Public Election Law Bill 2000). However, it was only with the end of the "Era of the Three Kims"[29] at the beginning of the new century that demands for reform in the name of efficiency finally affected the political class in their institutional sanctuary – the party chapters. The 2002 amendment of the PPA included the abolition of party liaison offices on the administrative levels of the towns (*ŭp*), townships (*myŏn*), and boroughs (*tong*), while the employment of salaried staff was once again allowed; however, this was limited to two members of staff per party chapter (see table A-2). It also allowed one paid member of staff in each liaison office at the level of districts (*ku*), cities (*si*), and counties (*kun*). The official reason for this revision was that it allowed for an "improvement of the organizational structure of political parties," as well as for the "promotion of a reasonable system of operating political parties" (PPA Bill 2002).

The following translations transpired during the time of the progressive government under Roh Moo-Hyun (No Mu-Hyŏn), who called his style of government "participatory government." Law amendments were treated as major issues of public concern, and the translation process evolved in a multitudinal, and open, manner. However, for various reasons, democratic principles no longer played the most important role in the political process, finding themselves outshone by the values of economic viability and efficiency (see Mosler 2012). Two years later, in 2004, the ambition to "abolish the system of party chapters for good" was justified on the grounds of wanting to tackle the problem of "the high-cost, low-efficiency structure of political parties," and of wanting to "create a new political climate, thereby advancing [Korean] political culture" (PPA Bill 2004). Moreover, the requirements for establishing a political party were made stricter. The required minimum number of party members was raised from about 700 to 5000 (see illustration 5–1). Here, the reasons

29 The expression "Three Kims' politics" usually designates Korean politics during the period of time in which major political leaders Kim Dae-Jung, Kim Young-Sam, and Kim Jong-Pil dominated the political landscape, that is, Korean politics in the period of time from the mid-1980s to the early 2000s.

stated make it clear that the main objective was no longer conceived in terms of democracy, but instead in terms of efficiency. Put differently, the reform discourse abandoned its political narrative, to be taken over by economically imbued storylines. Only one year later, another about-turn was to follow. The 2005 revision of the PPA re-installed basic party organization at the level of electoral districts for the general election and below, labeling them "members' councils" to make explicit their professed difference from the former party chapters. In terms of substance, however, they were the same entities, even though the members' councils were not granted official legal status. Moreover, the councils were under no obligation to register with the authorities, or to account for their activities in any other form. The reasoning advanced for this amendment spelled out aiming to "improve on and remedy certain deficiencies in the operation of the *current* system" (PPA Bill 2005; my emphasis). An analysis of the parliamentary sub-committee's meetings in 2005 reveals that this reform compromise was strongly influenced by the then predominant efficiency frame, which had only shortly before received additional boost from a decision by the constitutional court concerning the abolition of party chapters (see below). A recent revision was made in 2010, when the minimum number of applicants required for the registration of a central party branch was raised tenfold from 20 to 200, and from 10 to 100 for regional branches in provinces and cities (see table A-3). Without any further elaboration being advanced, this was officially done "to strengthen the requirements for the establishment of political parties" (PPA Bill 2010).

The illustration below summarizes only one aspect of the Political Parties Act's evolution over time and does so only in quantitative terms. However, in spite of the shortcomings of such drastic reduction down to only one dimension, it does have the merit of depicting tendencies in the development of translation over time. It shows that the obligatory minimum total number of party members has fallen steadily since the 1980s, a time when the strategy of the then authoritarian regime changed from direct control of the assembly (obvious manipulation) to more indirect means of control, taking the wind out of the sails of potential opposition forces precisely by letting them participate in satellite parties. This general trend toward a discourse of democracy continued, not surprisingly, under the "Civil Government" and the "Government of the People" of former opposition fighters for democracy Kim Young-Sam (1993~1998) and Kim Dae-Jung (1998~2003). It was only with the "Participatory Government" of Roh Moo-Hyun (2004~2008) that political parties were once again subjected to levels of regulation similar to those of the 1960s, a change that was justified with a *rhetoric of efficiency*.

Illustration 1: Obligatory minimum total number of party members (y) required for establishing a political party, 1962–today (x)[30]

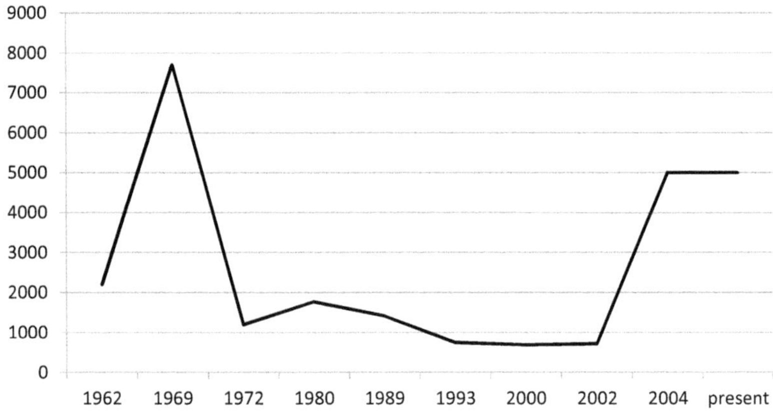

4.3 The vertical dimension – translations in the process of adjudication

In this last section I deal with vertical translations that are directly related to the question of changes in ideas and norms about political parties. "Vertical" here points to translations taking place on the way from the constitutional and other legal provisions on political parties as such to their actual application in the process of adjudication – that is to say, their interpretation. Two constitutional challenges were brought against the amendment of the Political Parties Act in 2004. While the rulings on these challenges deal with different provisions of the Political Parties Act, they both discuss the fundamental issue of the obligation to realize (intra-party) democracy on the one hand, and the freedom of political parties to choose their form of organization as stipulated in Article 8 of the Constitution on the other. A comparison of the lines of reasoning advanced in these two judgments relative to the Constitution and its meaning, coupled with a more general comparison of the two judgments, sheds much light on the process, and the subject matters, of adjudication on provisions relating to political parties.[31]

30 This illustration depicts the results of calculations made by the author on the basis of the figures contained in the PPA in relation to the number of electoral districts (see table A-3).

31 The following is only a rough summary of a more thorough comparison that I have conducted elsewhere (Mosler 2012a).

A. *Registration requirements for political parties*

The first constitutional review I shall examine here concerned the constitutionality of the strengthened registration requirements of the PPA (2004-hŏnma-246)[32]. According to the amended PPA, political parties had to have branches in at least five regional sub-divisions and a minimum of 5000 members in total, which equals about seven times the number of members required before the reform (see illustration 4–1 above). The Socialist Party filed a constitutional complaint in which it claimed that the respective provisions of the PPA hindered minor or newly established political parties from participating in party politics, thereby infringing upon the freedom of party formation under Article 8, Section 1, the right to equality under Article 11, and the freedom of association under Article 21, Section 1 of the Constitution. However, the complaint was rejected by the Court. The Court based its decision mainly on its finding that the articles in question aimed to exclude "regional" and "minor" political parties, and that doing so constituted "a legitimate legislative purpose" given that the "proper functioning of representative democracy under [the Korean] Constitution" required a "stable majority within the legislative branch" (Court 2006: 402f.).[33] In order to underpin the need to comply with these requirements, the Court directly and explicitly drew on the German Political Parties Act (PartG, Article 2, Section 1), which it read to mean that parties must be organized in such a way that they exist "permanently or for a lengthy period of time," are of "sufficient size and strength," and have a substantial presence "in the regions" (Court 2006: 413).[34] The Court apparently interpreted the Korean constitutional provision on political parties as requiring a solid and lasting organizational basis in the regions as a prerequisite to realizing the role assigned

---

32 The complaint was filed in March 2004, the court's decision was published in March 2006.

33 It declared that "[to exclude] regional parties from representing the political wills of only certain regions cannot be said to be an illegitimate purpose under the Constitution, when party politics depending excessively on regional affiliation has become problematic in our political reality" (Court 2006: 402f.).

34 It is an interesting, but probably coincidental, fact that the English *translation* of the decision omitted precisely those sentences that made explicit reference to the German Act. For example, the following sentence on page 218 of the Korean version is not included in the English translation: "In [...] addition to the requirements for political parties as set forth in Article 2 of the PPA, political parties shall meet the requirements contained in Article 2 of the German Political Parties Act, which states that 'parties permanently or for a lengthy period of time participate in the formation of the political will of the people.'" (my translation)

to political parties by the Constitution. This is obviously in keeping with German ideas and norms on this question, as well as with opinions advanced by a considerable number of domestic constitutional scholars (Mosler 2014).[35]

B. *The prohibition of party chapters*

The second constitutional review dealt with the constitutionality of the abolition of party chapters (2004-hŏnma-456).[36] The revised Political Parties Act prohibited party chapters or *chigudang*, that is, forms of party organization beneath the level of cities and provinces. Until then, party chapters had represented the smallest organizational units of political parties at the level of electoral districts for over forty years. However, many of them had been the scene of corruption and other forms of malpractice, and the general tenor of public debate, as reflected in the mass media, was one of repeated demands for reform to make political parties "less costly and more efficient." It was the Democratic Labor Party that finally brought the matter of the abolition of party chapters before the Constitutional Court. It argued that the relevant amended provisions of the PPA infringed upon the constitutionally granted freedom to establish political parties, including party sub-organizations, while at the same time contradicting the constitutional imperative of intra-party democracy. The Constitutional Court, however, unanimously struck down the challenge, mainly on the grounds that the amended Act did not, it held, violate *essential* aspects of the constitutionally granted freedom of political parties. However, closer analysis of the judgment reveals that the Court's ruling – while correct from a procedural point of view – ultimately fails to present a convincing line of reasoning (Mosler 2013). The interpretation of the Court was found to be rather 'law-unlike' (cf. Morawski 2004), particularly in light of the relative complexity of the constitutional norms related to political parties. The Court attributed too much weight to what is, in fact, only temporary election campaigning, as well as to the efficiency of political institutions, and the possibilities of modern-day transport and communication technology, and was, accordingly, misled into prematurely foreclosing the opportunity for upholding essential aspects of constitutional freedoms and rights.

---

35 That being so, designating the concrete number of "5000 members" as the number necessary to meet the rather abstract constitutional requirement of "realizing the role assigned by the Constitution," and excluding small parties on the basis of this, is, of course, going to remain controversial.

36 The complaint was filed in June 2004, and the decision made public in December 2004.

This was mainly due to the fact that it did not attribute sufficient weight to the kinds of readings of the constitutional provision on political parties that had been referred to in the judgment discussed above (2004-hŏnma-246), readings stressing sustainability and continuity, organizational arrangements sufficiently complex to allow for the effective and proportional participation of individuals, and genuine proximity to the electorate.

We can see that this second ruling was based on an argument directly opposed to the arguments advanced in the ruling discussed above, which had explicitly presented German law as providing authority for the Court's ruling. By ruling as it did on the question of party chapters, the Court can be said to have ignored relevant authority pointing in another direction, which includes having bypassed its own precedent. In addition, the Court also ruled contrary to the interpretations advanced by a large number of renowned constitutional scholars. It invoked the very interpretations it had relied on in the first decision discussed above, but this time in order to undermine them. As a result of these highly contradictory rulings by one and the same Court on one and the same constitutional provision, the actual contents of the Political Parties Act – amended as they were according to a standard of efficiency – were left untouched. What happened here can be summarized as "translation [taking] place within discourses in which some kinds of association or translation are legitimized and authorized just as others are excluded or denied" (Freeman 2009: 434).

5. Findings

One of the aims of this chapter was to contribute to the developing field of studies examining the circulation of legal ideas and norms through the lense of translation. Mindful of the manner in which the policy translation literature partly developed by distinguishing itself from the policy transfer perspective, I have tried to highlight the strengths of the legal translation metaphor by disentangling it from the metaphor of legal transplantation. By shifting from transplantation to translation in my analysis of acts of legal transfer, I have discovered a potential in the concept of legal translation that is akin to the potential of policy translation as already evidenced by a steadily growing amount of policy translation literature. Established metaphors such as those of legal transplant, legal irritant, or legal transformation are useful in their own right; yet, as was shown above, the translation metaphor allows for a potentially wider and deeper epistemological perception of the phenomena associated with the circulation of legal ideas. This is mainly due to the fact that the metaphor of translation naturally lends itself to ontological post-positivistic interpretivism. As a result of this turn toward interpretivism, the metaphorical device of legal translation does not content itself with painting a one-dimensional picture of the supposedly simple movement of an object from here to there, but instead assumes a multilayered process that involves the (re-)creation of ideas and norms in various dimensions. No doubt, there is still much room left for debate, for example with regard to alternative metaphors such as that of *transcoding*.[37] However, what should have become obvious by now is that it is necessary to take off the blinkers inspired by the natural sciences and try to gain a better understanding of the discursive dynamics as they can be found especially in processes of policy and law making.

Another consequence of the post-positivistic turn involves the step from metaphor to method. The second aim of this chapter was to test the explanatory power of the translation metaphor by demonstrating its practical applicability. Due mainly to the basic interpretivist assumptions underlying the analytical arsenal of ideational approaches such as discursive institutionalism (DI) or argumentative discourse analysis (ADA), it was possible to make use of these very approaches in sublimating the translation metaphor into a methodological approach apt for empirical analysis. Making policy or legal norms inevitably involves certain structures, institutions, and actors that have to be taken into account when analyzing these processes of creation. For politicians as well as for lawyers, judges, and scholars of legal language, words and speech (or writing) constitute the central medium, while communication, together with negotiation and persuasion, constitutes the most important practice. While those who engage in discourse competition inevitably do so with certain aims in mind, the outcomes of using the aforementioned media and engaging in the aforementioned practices are rarely identical with what the actors intended to achieve. This is why we have to look into these contentious interactions from an analytical perspective, examining the various meta-layers, looking behind the words and their meanings and delving into their construction.

Empirical analysis of the legal norms and ideas concerning political parties in Korea reveals that, by virtue of being geared towards domestic purposes, they had been shaped by specific domestic interests and domestic negotiations of those interests. Even though I have applied my suggestion for a novel methodological approach to a selected number of exemplary cases only, future comparisons

37 Professor Marion Eggert from the Department of Korean Studies at Ruhr University Bochum introduced this term while chairing one of the panel discussions at the "Lost and Found" conference, explaining that a research project at Bochum university had started to speak of "transcoding," rather than "translating," on the grounds that "transcoding" had the benefit of being more abstract.

involving different countries, times, and interpretations are sure to reveal the full explanatory power of the translational metaphor. My findings can be summarized as follows: The horizontal translation of German party law in 1960s Korea was monopolized by the then authoritarian regime. At first sight, the resulting legal code seems to have turned its role model upside down, but it was, in actual fact, a "Korean-style" creation, designed to fit the historical Korean context. Diagonal translation developed over time on the basis of monopolized translations in the 1970s and 1980s. The plot had become slightly different by then, but the story that was told was still the same, and this was to remain true throughout the period of the oligopolized translations of the 1990s, when the story changed to one of formal democracy. Finally, multi-polarized translations emerged at the beginning of the 21st century, influenced by neoliberal trends and their narratives of efficiency. The vertical translations represented by the Constitutional Court's rulings of 2004 and 2006 bear the distinct marks of the discourse of efficiency, which by then had become hegemonic.

6. Discussion

What are the implications of these findings? Wherein lies the value of the new perspective? What is there to learn from applying the analytical tools it offers? I would like to stress two aspects here. First, there is a clear need to design and execute processes of legal decision making in such a way that they will be more democratic and less technocratic. However, so long as legal norms are thought of as transplants, the best that can be hoped for in terms of legal decision making is a bit of tinkering with the fictitious "legal machine," using whatever spare parts one happens to have come across. Such tinkering, of course, will never get to the actual roots of legal, political, social, economic, and other obstacles in the way of Korea's "development," instead playing only with the symptoms. The foregoing analysis shows that even after the formal democratization of the late 1980s, and the opening up of the arena of institutionalized politics to civil society in the late 1990s, reforms of laws on political parties continued to be carried out in accordance with a mindset of prescriptive control, which, as we just saw, was the result of pre-established mechanisms and dynamics. The analysis revealed that despite frequent and often substantial changes, it is possible to discern an intriguing continuity between the various translations, which all shared the following common features: (a) regular recourse to German provisions on political parties as *authoritative*legal references and sources of *authority*; (b) a line of reasoning that draws on narratives of efficiency to assert *authority*; and (c) the regulation of party politics in an *authoritarian* and prescriptive manner. Second, and relatedly, the solution is not to understand translation as the transplantation of a high quantity of high-quality foreign ideas and norms, but as a critical, self-reflective, and creative piece of work that also draws on the immediate environment in all its puzzling complexity. This is in keeping with a recent trend in the field of political science in Korea, which has expressed a clear demand to focus less on potential foreign imports and more on a detailed assessment of domestic needs (Hahm 2001; Bae 2003; Han 2003; Kim 2008; Lim 2010).

One example of this novel kind of work is the critical research done by Chaihark Hahm, who contends that constitutional discourse in Korea is isolated from Korean cultural and political tradition, while it is, in fact, vital for constitutionalism, if it is to flourish, to be connected to and grounded in close and consistent references to both culture and politics (Hahm 2001: 156, 193f.). Short of such referencing, Hahm maintains, Korean constitutionalism "will always remain a 'derivative' practice, an epiphenomenon dependent on the constitutional experiences of Germans or Americans" (Hahm 2001: 193f.). To provide a practical illustration of how to achieve such an authentic reference capable of supporting a functional, modern form of constitutionalism, Hahm highlights the concept of *ye* or ritual, which he describes as an ancient constitutional norm that should be "retrieved and *translated* into a modern context" (Hahm 2001: 196; my emphasis).

> Korean constitutionalism will flourish when the citizens of Korea are able to make an outcast of a political leader who fails to observe the requirements of *ye*, when a government that fails to be disciplined in the exercise of its power will automatically be regarded as illegitimate (Hahm 2001: 196).

Another example for novel strands in Korean scholarship is an article by Byungsam Bae titled "Search of the Origin and Identity of Korean Politics," in which Bae argues that contemporary Korean political science is stuck in its colonial legacies. According to him, there is a need to locate the origins of Korean political science nowhere else but in the Korean tradition itself. In proposing the creation of a "new origin," Bae draws on Hobsbawm and Ranger's "The Invention of Tradition" (1984), arguing that culture and scholarship develop reciprocally, and that "tradition" had no independent existence prior to its invention during the process of modernization (Bae 2003: 103). For Bae, delving into Korea's past in order to "recreate Korean political science" is not only necessary, but justified. His practical suggestions for how to succeed in doing so rely on reviving the ancient ideal of virtuous rule or *tŏkji*, which, to him, practically translates into "listening carefully" (Bae 2003: 99).

> Here the identity of "listening carefully" can be adopted for […] the purposes of modern Korean political science. Not only that, […] a "political science of listening carefully" can

> also be sublimated into a universal concept, since it has a close affinity to post-modernist thought as it is currently developed in the West (Bae 2003: 103; my translation).

In a similar vein, Sung-hack Lim's article engages in a self-critique of Korean political science, which, he maintains, has failed to develop a specifically Korean identity in spite of its recent growth in diversity and scale (Lim 2010: 257). While his work focuses on the finding that Korean political science needs to open up to methodological diversity and plurality of authorship, Lim also emphasizes the importance of "*creating* a Korean political science that can explain Korean reality" (Lim 2010: 272; my translation and emphasis). In doing so, he does not make the mistake of focusing on "Koreanness" down to the point of adopting a nationalistic perspective. This view on Korean political science is shared by Bae-ho Han, who in his critical "review of Korean political science" maintains that the identity and autonomy of the latter go hand in hand with its ability to explain Korean reality and with the liveliness of the exchanges among Korean scholars in the field (Han 2003: 75).

In an article from 2008, Yong-ho Kim reflects on the Korean scholarship regarding political parties and proposes a way of strengthening its identity (Kim 2008). He contends that in spite of the considerable volume of criticisms and proposals concerning the identity of Korean social science in the last three decades, and in spite of recent attempts to break with old habits, Korean social science is still looking through a Western-centric prism (Kim 2008: 66). According to him, it is now time to free Korean scholarship on political parties from what is essentially a top-down method of trying to explain Korean parties with Western theory, and to instead adopt a bottom-up method of first observing and analyzing the reality of Korean political parties, and then developing general theories only as a second step (Kim 2008: 75).

> Just as Western theory did not fall from the heavens but was created on the basis of observations of the realities of Western political parties, we, too, must first observe, in detail and systematically, and over an extended period of time, the actions of party leaders, party cadres, members, supporters, and of the electorate, and then proceed to building theory. In order to do so, we have to analyze why [these protagonists] act as they do in politico-psychological and politico-anthropological terms (Kim 2008: 75; my translation).

All these examples of recent scholarship go to show that there is a self-critical awareness developing in Korean academia concerning the origin, identity, and future of Korean scholarship. They concur in finding that Korean social science suffers from a lack of autonomy, be it due to obstruction by Japanese influences since the end of the 20th century, or due to US-American or Western influences since the 1940s, or both. Finally, they all seem to share the view that the solution to the problem lies in building "something of their own," something "autochthonous", all the while being cautious not to adopt narrow-minded, nationalistic tones. While Hahm (2001) explicitly speaks of "translating" tradition into modern contexts, Bae (2003) advocates "sublimating" ancient ideals into universal concepts. Lim (2010), Han (2003), and Kim (2008) all seem to agree on the need to "create" something that can be called "Korean political science," and to "build" theory by way of induction from Korean reality, thus rejecting the idea of exclusively relying on deductions from Western theory. These examples reveal two important facts. The literature agrees on the necessity of becoming more active, of no longer being "at the receiving end." It also stresses the importance of focusing on the specificity of domestic, Korean needs, and of choosing research modes and mindsets accordingly.

Korean policy and law have no doubt always been "Made in Korea." The question of whether the relevant processes of making policy and laws can more aptly characterized as "original" or "derivative" in nature should not divert attention from the far more pressing question of how such processes should be designed and conducted in the future. It is my understanding that the translation metaphor as an analytical tool is capable of providing valuable clues to identifying, and ultimately meeting, the challenges ahead in making policy and laws in Korea.

References

Bae, Byung-sam. 2003. "Han'guk chŏngch'ihak-ŭi kiwon-kwa chŏngch'esŏng t'amsaek [In search of the origins and identity of Korean political science]," *Han'gukjŏngch'ihakhoebo* ch'ilsipsam-chib, iho [Journal of the Korean Association for Political Science, Vol. 37, No.], 87–105.

Choi, Chongko. 1981. "On the reception of Western law in Korea," *Korean Journal of Comparative Law*, Vol. 9. 141–167.

Constitutional Court of the Republic of Korea. 2006. "Chŏngdangbŏp che-25-cho tŭng-ŭi wihŏnsŏng-e taehan kyŏlchŏng" [Judgment on the unconstitutionality of Article 25 etc. of the Political Parties Act]. *Hŏnbŏpchaep'anso kyŏlchŏngmun [18 Constitutional Court Decision Collection]*, 402–416.

Czarniawska, B. and Joerges, B. 1996. "Travels of ideas." *Translating Organizational Change*. Edited by B. Czarniawska and G. Sevon. Berlin: Walter de Gruyter, 13–48.

Evans, Peter. 2003. "Development as Institutional Change: The Pitfalls of Monocropping and the Potentials of Deliberation." *Studies in Comparative International Development*, Vol. 38, No. 4. 30–52.

Ewald, William. 1995. "Comparative Jurisprudence (II): The Logic of Legal Transplants," *American Comparative Law*, Vol. 43, No. 4, 489–510.

Fadé, Lujo. 1993. "Rechtstransfer nach Osteuropa – eine Investition in die Zukunft." *Wirtschaft und Recht in Osteuropa*, Vol. 2, No. 3. 87–89.

Freeman, Richard. 2009. *"What is 'translation'?" Evidence & Policy* Vol. 5, No. 4. 429–447.

Freeman, Richard. 2006. "Policy Moves: Translation, Policy and Politics." University of Edinburgh, Typescript.

Ginsburg, Tom 2010. "The Constitutional Court and the Judicialization of Korean Politics," In Andrew Harding and Penelope Nicholson (eds.). *New Courts in Asia*. New York: Routledge.

Hahm, Chaihark. 2001. "Conceptualizing Korean Constitutionalism: Foreign Transplant or Indigenous Tradition?" *Journal of Korean Law*, Vol. 1, No. 2. 151–196.

Hahm, Pyong-Choon. 1971. *The Korean Political Tradition and Law*. Seoul: Hollym Corporation Publishers.

Hajer, Maarten. 1995. *The Politics of Environmental Discourse: Ecological Modernization and the Policy Process*. New York: Clarendon Press.

Hajer, Maarten. 1997. *The Politics of Environmental Discourse: Ecological Modernization and the Policy Process*. Oxford: Oxford University Press.

Hajer, Maarten. 2003. "Argumentative Diskursanalyse. Auf der Suche nach Koalitionen, Praktiken und Bedeutung." In *Handbuch Sozialwissenschaftliche Diskursanalyse, Forschungspraxis*. Edited by Keller, R./Hirseland, A./Schneider, W./Viehöfer, W. (ed.). Opladen: Leske + Budrich (Bd. 2), 271–298.

Hajer, Maarten. 2008. "Diskursanalyse in der Praxis: Koalitionen, Praktiken und Bedeutung." In *Die Zukunft der Policy-Forschung. Theorien, Methoden, Anwendungen*. Edited by Janning, Frank/Katrin Toens, Wiesbaden: VS-Verlag, 211–222.

Han, Bae-ho. 2003. "Han'gukjŏngch'hak haksa: ch'ongnon [The History of Korean Political Science: An Outline]," Han'gukjŏngch'ihakhoe (Ed.). Han'gukjŏngch'ihakhoe-osib-nyŏnsa: 1953–2003 [Fifty Years of the Korean Association for Political Science: 1953–2003]. Seoul: Han'gukjŏngch'hakhoe.

Huntington, Samuel P. 1968. *Political Order in Changing Societies*. New Haven: University Press.

Janda, Kenneth. 2005. *Political Parties and Democracy in Theoretical and Practical Perspectives. Adopting Party Law*. Washington, D.C.: National Democratic Institute for International Affairs.

Kahn-Freund, Otto. 1974. "On Uses and Misuses of Comparative Law." *Mod.L.Rev.*, Vol. 37, No. 1. 1–27.

Kang, Won-Taek. 2005. *Han'guk-ŭi chŏngch'igaehyŏk-kwa minjujuŭi [Political reform and democracy in Korea]*. Seoul: In'gansarang.

Kang, Jung In. 2011. "An Analysis of Park Chung-hee's Discourses on Democracy: Focusing on his 'Administrative', 'National' and 'Korean-style' Democracy." *Sogang Journal of Philosophy*, Vol. 27, Nov 2011. 287–321.

Katz, Richard S. and Peter Mair. 1995. "Changing Models of Party Organization and Party Democracy: The Emergence of the Cartel Party." *Party Politics*, Vol. 1, No. 1 (January 1995). 5–28.

Kim, Hyo-jŏn. 1985. "Hangug-e issŏsŏ togil hŏnbŏp iron-ŭi ch'ogi suyong [The initial adoption of German constitutional theory in Korea]," *Tonga taehakkyo taehakwon nonmunjip*, Vol. 2. 108–142.

Kim, Hyo-jŏn. 2003. „Hangug-esŏ togil kongbŏp iron-ŭi yŏnghyang [The influence of German theories of public law in Korea], *Handokpŏphak*, Vol. 14. 331–379.

Young Huh. 1977. „Begegnung europäischer und ostasiatischer Rechtskultur," *Verfassung und Recht in Übersee*, Vol. 10.

Kim, Kyun and Wŏn-kŭn Song. 2000. "Chaebŏl kaehyŏk-ŭi kkŭt: p'ŏngga-wa chŏnmang [The end of the chaebol reform: evaluation and prospects]," *Tonghyang-kwa chŏnmang [Trends and Prospects]*, sasipsa-ho pom [Vol. 44, Spring]. 101–121.

Kim, Yong-Ho. 1989. *Authoritarian Leadership and Party Dynamics: The Rise and Fall of the Democratic Republican Party in South Korea, 1962–1980*. PhD. University of Pennsylvania.

Kim Yong-Ho. 1992. "Authoritarian Leadership and Hegemonic Party Building: A Comparative Analysis of Mexico and South Korea." *Asian Perspective*. Vol. 10, Nr. 16. Fall-Winter 1992. 83–108.

Kim Yong-Ho. 2008. "Han'gukjŏngdang yŏn'gu-ŭi hangmun-chŏk chŏngch'esŏng hwangnip-ŭl wihan sŏngch'al [Reflections on the Discipline of Korean Party Studies for Building Up Its Academic Identity]," *Han'gukjŏngdanghakhoebo*, che-ch'il-kwon, che-i-ho, t'onggwon-sipsam-ho [*Journal of the Korean Association for Political Party Studies*, Vol, 7, No. 2, Serial 13]. 65–81.

Kwantes, Johan. 2010. "The Idea Behind the Constitution: an interview with Chaihark Hahm," NIAS Newsletter, 19.01.2010. 10–14.

Kwŏn, Yŏng-Sŏn. 1998. *Hŏnbŏphakwŏllon [Constitutional Theory]*. Seoul: Bŏmmunsa.

Langer, Maximo. 2004. "From Legal Transplants to Legal Translations: The Globalization of Plea Bargaining and the Americanization Thesis in Criminal Procedure." *Harvard International Law Journal*, Vol. 45, No. 1. 1–64.

Lee, Duk-Yeon. 2007. *Tamnon-kwa haesŏk: hŏnboppyŏngnonjip [Discourse and Interpretation: Constitutional Reviews]*. Seoul: Isibil-segigyoyuksa.

Legrand, Pierre. 1997. "The Impossibility of Legal Transplants." *Maastricht J. European & Comparative Law 110.*

Lim, Sung-hack. 2010. "Han'guk chŏngch'hak yŏn'gu-ŭi tonghyang-kwa chŏngch'esŏng hwangnip-ŭl wihan taean [Trends in Korean Political Science and Proposals for its Improvement]," *Chŏngch'i chŏngboyŏn'gu*, che-sipsam-kwon che-i-ho [*Research on Politics and Information*, Vol. 13, No. 2]. 257–274.

Mosler, Hannes B. 2012. "Curtailing political parties with efficiency: the policy decision to abolish party chapters in South Korea." *ASIEN* 125. 8–34.

Mosler, Hannes B. 2013. *Sarajin chigudang, kongjŏng-hanŭn chŏngdang kaehyŏk [Party district chapters disappeared, party reform idling]*. Koyang: In'gansarang.

Mosler, Hannes B. 2014. "Judicialization of Politics and the Korean Constitutional Court: the *Party Chapter Abolition Case*," *Zeitschrift für Verfassung und Recht in Übersee*, 47. Jahrgang, Heft 3. 292–317.

Morawski, Lech. 2004. "Stressing – The Controversy between Judicial Passivism and Activism", In: T. Biernat and others (Hrsg.). *Stressing Legal Decisions.* Cracow.

Müller, Friedrich, Ralph Christensen und Michael Sokolowski. 1989. *Rechtstext und Textarbeit.* Berlin: Duncker & Humboldt.

von Münch, Ingo. 1994. "Rechtsexport und Rechtsimport." *Neue Juristische Wochenschrift,* Heft 48, 3146–7.

Orücü, Esin. 2002. "Law as Transposition." *International & Comparative Law Quarterly* 51: 205.

Park, Chung-Hee. 1962. *Ŭri minjŏk-ŭi naagal kil [Der Weg unseres Volkes]*. Seoul: Tongach'ulp'ansa.

Park, Chung-Hee. 1963. *Kukka-wa hyŏngmyŏng-kwa na [Der Staat, die Revolution und ich]*. Seoul: Hyangmunsa.

Park, Sang-Hun. 2004. "Chibaedamnonhwadoen chŏngch'igaehyŏk-kwa minjujuŭi." [Political reform as hegemonic discourse and democracy], *Irongwa silch'ŏn* [Theory and Reality] (February/March). 170–181.

Peerenboom, Randy. 2012. "Toward a Methodology for Successful Legal Transplants." *Working Paper Series*, La Trobe University, Faculty of Law and Management; Oxford University Centre for Socio-Legal Studies.

Pistor, Katharina and Phillip Wellons. 1999. *The Role of Law and Legal Institutions in Asian Economic Development 1960–1995*. New York: Oxford University Press.

Potter, Pitman B. 2004. "Legal Reform in China: Institutions, Culture, and Selective Adaptation." *Law & Social Inquiry* 29, 465.

Rehm, Gebhard M. 2008. "Rechtsplantate als Instrument der Rechtsreform und –transformation." *RabelsZ*, Bd. 72. 1–42.

Schmidt, Vivien. 2002. *The Futures of European Capitalism*. Oxford, UK: Oxford University Press.

Schmidt, Vivien. 2008. "Discursive Institutionalism: The Explanatory Power of Ideas and Discourse." *Annual Review of Political Science*, Vol. 11. 303–326.

Schmidt, Vivien. 2010. "Taking ideas and discourse seriously: explaining change through discursive institutionalism as the fourth 'new institutionalism.'" *European Political Science Review*, Vol. 2, No. 1. 1–25.

Song, Seog-Yun. 2000. "Togilhŏnbŏpsang chŏngdangjohang-kwa kŭ han'guk-chŏk isik. Pigyobŏpsahoehak-chŏk chŏpkŭn" [The German Constitutional Provision on Political Parties and its Transplantation to Korea: A Comparative Socio-Legal Approach], Sŏuldaehakkyo pŏphak [41 Seoul National University Law Journal]. 115–146.

Teubner, Gunter. 1998. "Legal Irritants: good faith in British Law or how unifying law ends up in new divergences." *Modern Law Review,* Vol. 61. 11–32.

Viehöver, Willy. 2006. "Die Wissenschaft und die Wiederbezauberung des sublunaren Raumes. Der Klimadiskurs im Licht der narrativen Diskursanalyse." In *Handbuch Sozialwissenschaftliche Diskursanalyse,* eds. Keller, R./Hirseland, A./Schneider, W./Viehöfer, W., Forschungspraxis, Opladen: Leske + Budrich.

Watson, Alan. 1974. *Legal Transplants – An Approach to Comparative Law*. Edinburgh: Scottish Academic Press.

White, James Boyd. 1990. *Justice as translation: An essay in cultural and legal criticism*. Chicago: University of Chicago Press.

Xu, Zhangrun. 2004. "Western Law in China: transplantation or transformation – four cases and Liang Shuming's responses." *Social Sciences in China*, Vol. 25. 3–27.

Yu, Ŭn-Hyŏn. 1974. "Han'guk-jŏk minjujuŭi-ŭi olbarŭn ihae-wa silch'ŏn: minjujuŭi chŏnghyŏngnaeyong" [The correct understanding and realization of Korean Democracy: standard contents of democracy], *Kyŭngch'al Kosi*, Vol. 114(74.4). 28–33.

Laws cited

Assembly Member Election Act (AMEA), 1988

Constitution of the Republic of Korea (Constitution), 1987

Gesetz über die politischen Parteien (Political Parties Act – PartG), 1967

Grundgesetz der Bundesrepublik Deutschland (Basic Law – GG), 1949

Political Parties Act (PPA), 1962

Political Parties Act (PPA), 2004

Political Parties Act (PPA), 2005

Public Election Law (PEL), 2004

Bills Cited

Assembly Member Election Act Bill (AMEAB), 1988

Political Parties Act Bill (PPB), 1963

Political Parties Act Bill (PPB), 1969

Political Parties Act Bill (PPB), 1972

Political Parties Act Bill (PPB), 1980

Political Parties Act Bill (PPB), 1989

Political Parties Act Bill (PPB), 1993

Political Parties Act Bill (PPB), 2000

Political Parties Act Bill (PPB), 2002

Political Parties Act Bill (PPB), 2004

Political Parties Act Bill (PPB), 2005

Political Parties Act Bill (PPB), 2010

Decisions Cited

2004-hŏnma-246 (March 30, 2006)

2004-hŏnma-456 (December 16, 2004)

Appendix

*Table A-1: Changes in the Constitutional Provision on Political Parties (1960 ~ 1987)**

1960	1963	1972	1980	1987
Article 13	**Article 7**	**Article 7**	**Article 7**	**Article 8**
All people shall not receive restrictions in their freedom of speech, to assemble, and to publish. Political parties enjoy the protection of the State as prescribed by law. But, if the objectives or activities of a political party are contrary to the Constitution's fundamental democratic order, the Government may bring action against it by obtaining the approval of the president, and the dissolution of the party is ordered through the decision of the Constitutional Court.	(1) **The establishment of political parties is free, and a plural party system is guaranteed.** (2) **Political parties must be democratic in their organization and activities and they must have the necessary organization to participate in the formation of the political will of the people.** (3) Political parties enjoy the protection of the State **[...]**. But, if the objectives or activities of a political party are contrary to the fundamental democratic order, the Government	(1) The establishment of political parties is free, and a plural party system is guaranteed. (2) Political parties must be democratic in their organization and activities and they must have the necessary organization to participate in the formation of the political will of the people. (3) Political parties enjoy the protection of the State as prescribed by law. But, if the objectives or activities of a political party are contrary to the fundamental democratic order **or endanger the existence of the state,** the Government may bring action against it in the	(1) The establishment of political parties is free, and a plural party system is guaranteed. (2) Political parties must be democratic in their organization and activities and they must have the necessary organization to participate in the formation of the political will of the people. (3) Political parties enjoy the protection of the State **and may be provided with operational funds by the State under the conditions as prescribed by law.**	(1) The establishment of political parties is free, and a plural party system is guaranteed. (2) Political parties must be democratic in their **objectives,** organization, and activities and they must have the necessary organization to participate in the formation of the political will of the people. (3) Political parties enjoy the protection of the State and may be provided with operational funds by the State under the conditions as prescribed by law.

1960	1963	1972	1980	1987
Article 13	**Article 7**	**Article 7**	**Article 7**	**Article 8**
	may bring action against it [...] in the **Supreme Court** for its dissolution, and, the political party is dissolved in accordance with the decision of the **Supreme Court**.	**Constitutional Committee** for its dissolution, and, the political party is dissolved in accordance with the decision of the **Constitutional Committee**.		
			(4) If the objectives or activities of a political party are contrary to the fundamental democratic order [...], the Government may bring action against it in the **Constitutional Committee** for its dissolution, and, the political party is dissolved in accordance with the decision of the **Constitutional Committee.**	(4) If the objectives or activities of a political party are contrary to the fundamental democratic order, the Government may bring action against it in the **Constitutional Court** for its dissolution, and, the political party is dissolved in accordance with the decision of the **Constitutional Court.**

Note: "[…]" denotes deleted phrases or passages.

Table A-2: Changes in selected articles of the South Korean Political Parties Act (1962 ~ 2002)

Year	Obligatory constituent units			Optional constituent units	
	central party	regional branches	local chapters	liaison offices	
1962	*capitol (Seoul)*	(provinces and cities)	*general election districts*	(cities, counties)	×
1972	*capitol (Seoul)*	(provinces and cities)	*general election districts*	(districts, cities, counties)	×
1980	*capitol (Seoul)*	(provinces and cities)	*general election districts*	(districts, cities, counties)	[open]
1989	*capitol (Seoul)*	(provinces and cities)	*general election districts*	(districts, cities, counties)	(town, township, borough)
2002	*capitol (Seoul)*	(provinces and cities)	*general election districts*	(districts, cities, counties)	[open]
2004	*capitol (Seoul)*	*provinces and cities**	×	×	×
2005	*capitol (Seoul)*	*provinces and cities**	(general election districts)*	(districts, cities, counties)	(town, township, borough)

Note:
Constituent units in italics are stipulated by law, i.e., are indispensable to establishing and running a party.
Constituent units in parenthesis are optional, i.e., it is up to the party to decide whether or not to have them.
Constituent units marked with an "**×**"are explicitly or implicitly forbidden by law.
Constituent units marked with "[open]" are open to legal interpretation.
* According to Article 37 (freedom of activities) of the PPA, only "members' councils" are allowed, while it is forbidden to operate offices. Members' councils have no legal capacity, nor do they have a duty to report to the authorities (as opposed to the "local chapters").

Table A-3: Obligatory and optional constituent units of political parties (PPA, §4 / 1962 ~ 2010)

Kind of prescription	More detailed contents		Year of amendment to the Political Parties Act								
		1962	1969	1972	1980	1989	1993	2000	2002	2004*	2010
minimum number of initiators**	in the central party	30	30	30	20	20	20	20	20	20	200
	per party chapter	10	10	10	10	10	10	10	10	10	100
minimum requirements for establishment of political parties (Article 4)	party chapter dispersion rate***	5	5	3	5	5	5	5	5	5	5
	number of party chapters****	1/3	1/2	1/3	1/4	1/5	1/10	1/10	1/10	1/50	1/50
	*number of direct election districts (total number of seats)******	*131 (175)*	*153 (204)*	*73 (219)*	*184 (276)*	*237 (299)*	*253 (299)*	*227 (273)*	*243 (273)*	*245 (299)*	*246 (299)*
	total number of party chapters	*44*	*77*	*24*	*46*	*47*	*24*	*23*	*24*	*5*	*5*
	number of individual party chapter members******	50	100	50	30	30	30	30	30	1000	1000
	total number of party chapter members	*2200*	*7700*	*1200*	*1770*	*1410*	*750*	*690*	*720*	*5000*	*5000*

* Relating not to party chapters, but to city/province parties (according to the 2004 amendment) (KPartG 2004).

** According to KPartG 2002, Article 5. (in 2012 it's article 6)

*** umber of party chapters dispersed over special municipal cities, municipal cities, and provinces (KPartG 2002, Article 26).

**** Relative number of party chapters against total number of assemblymen election districts (KPartG 2002, Article 25).

***** As of the date of the following general elections, 1963, 1971, 1973, 1981, 1992, 1996, 2000, 2002, 2004, 2012, respectively.

****** According to KPartG 2002, Article 27.

Research on Korea

Edited by Marion Eggert, Eun-Jeung Lee and Jörg Plassen

Volume 1 Marion Eggert / Felix Siegmund / Dennis Würthner (eds.): Space and Location in the Circulation of Knowledge (1400–1800). Korea and Beyond. 2014.

Volume 2 Eun-Jeung Lee / Hannes B. Mosler (eds.): Lost and Found in *Translation.* Circulating Ideas of Policy and Legal Decision Processes in Korea and Germany. 2015.

www.peterlang.com

www.ingramcontent.com/pod-product-compliance
Ingram Content Group UK Ltd.
Pitfield, Milton Keynes, MK11 3LW, UK
UKHW021833100926
8556IPUK00004B/309

9 783631 649084